The Family Care Roadmap

By Steve Edwards

Forever Family

Copyright © Family Concerns LLC
1999 Distributed by Forever Family Marketing

A NOTE TO THE READER

"The Family Care Roadmap" is a self-help document intended to provide families with a centralized source of information regarding family care and support. It is not designed to replace the need for insurance coverage or legal and financial documentation such as Advanced Directives and Trusts. It is highly advised that you share both the information contained within this book and your decisions with your professional advisors. This enables them to better serve your family's interests.

Quantity discounts are available for "The Family Care Roadmap" when used to promote products or services. For information, please call 1-800-308-8565.

LIBRARY OF CONGRESS CATALOGING IN PUBLICATION DATA

Edwards, Steve.

The Family Care Roadmap by Steve Edwards.

ISBN 1-928679-01-3

Cover Design by Norman Johnson
Layout/Graphic Design by Kim Wilks

Printed in the United States of America

Published by:

Forever Family Marketing
1340 Main Street, Suite 190
Grapevine, Texas 76051
800-308-8565

Forever Family

The Family Care Roadmap

Preparing for the Trip: Page

The Trip Begins:

Introducing Your Tour Guide

Steve Edwards, President of Family Concerns, has had years of consulting experience with corporations and health care agencies, as well as with the elderly and their families regarding aging and care issues.

As minister of a large church and director of a multi-service health care and social services agency, each for over a decade, his credits also include producing a weekly nationally syndicated TV series on aging, caregiving and home care issues. He's also written a weekly newspaper column, hosted a radio show and conducted numerous seminars on family care topics. As a recognized authority, he has appeared on numerous national TV and radio shows, including Phil Donahue and Discovery Channel.

Mr. Edwards is a published author, featured speaker* and frequent contributor to national magazines and newspapers. He is the author/producer of **"The Family Care Builder Series"** including **"The Family Care Roadmap", "The Family Care Organizer"** and producer/writer/host of **"The Family Care Video Series".**

* Call 800-308-8565 to schedule Steve Edwards as a featured speaker or seminar leader.

Getting Oriented

Getting Oriented

Welcome to **"The Family Care Roadmap"**. As you read the **"Roadmap"**, you'll be taken on a journey that leads you to a number of family care destinations.

Because family care impacts virtually every area of your life, taking charge of personal decisions and wishes becomes critical. The same holds true for every family member. This means personal planning and preparedness! Organizing your affairs! Communicating your wishes! Building a family and professional support network!

This is valid for every household in America, regardless of age or marital status.

But, to achieve the desired results, whether you're currently working or retired, takes time and effort. It requires that you develop a plan and work toward it.

Story

There's the story of a man, who walked into a French restaurant in New York City and ordered a lobster dinner. The waiter brought out the dinner. But, the man noticed that the lobster had no claws. He said, "waiter, come here." When the waiter arrived, he said, "Look at this lobster. It has no claws." To which the waiter replied, "Sir, our lobsters are so fresh, they fight each other." The man picked up his plate and said, "Then take this one back. Bring me a winner."

Family care is not about winning. But, it is about losing. Without preparedness both you and your family run the risk of losing:

- Personal Security
- Peace of Mind
- Control over Decisions
- Home
- Thousands of Dollars
- Independence
- Family Unity

This is NOT what I want!

The key to family care? It's planning, organizing, and communicating your wishes. It's also commitment. Your commitment to yourself, your family and others.

Your family care journey via **"The Family Care Roadmap"** will take you to many interesting destinations. These tour stops will greatly assist both you and your family in learning about and preparing for family care.

6

Packing For Your TRIP

Packing For Your Trip

Your family care journey will be a unique kind of trip. No, there won't be the traditional chips, dips, drinks and insect repellent. Instead, you'll be utilizing products from **"The Family Care Builder Series"**.

This is what I want!

GOOD NEWS!!

In fact, this trip is "all inclusive". Everything you need is included. With this in mind, let's do a quick inventory of what's in **"The Family Care Builder Series"**:

"The Family Care Builder Series" includes **"The Family Care Roadmap"**, **"The Family Care Organizer"** and **"The Family Care Video Series"**.

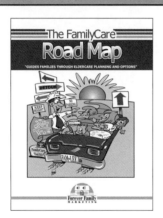

The Products

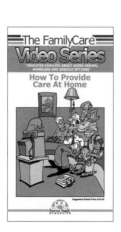

"The Family Care Builder Series" is nationally recommended by attorneys, clergy, financial planners, health care experts and social workers.

"The Family Care Roadmap"

The Family Care Builder Series

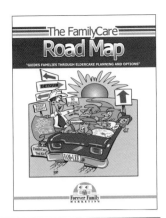

As your family's roadmap to professional and community resources, homecare and eldercare information, **"The Family Care Roadmap"** offers a wealth of practical and caring information. The **"Roadmap"** features sections on "Home Health Care", "Family Care", "Long Term Care", "Housing Options", "Estate Planning" and much more. It serves as a companion to **"The Family Care Organizer"** and **"The Family Care Video Series"**.

Benefits of "The Family Care Roadmap"

- Increases your family's understanding of the importance of preparedness planning and communication.
- Educates your family about essential financial, medical and legal decisions, care options, community services and professionals.
- Creates awareness for family members regarding caregiving, housing, and long-term care trends.
- Offers families a roadmap to resources and estate planning.

"The Family Care Organizer"

The Family Care Builder Series

As a very important solution to planning, organizing and communicating your affairs, family experts highly recommend that every household in America, regardless of age or marital status, complete **"The Family Care Organizer"**. It's today's most comprehensive way for both you and your family members to make decisions, convey wishes and organize vitally important information before a need, crisis or extended health concern occurs.

Easy to complete, this fill-in-the-blank guide provides the outline for both individual and family preparedness planning.

Benefits of "The Family Care Organizer"

- Organizes, plans and communicates essential family decisions.
- Builds a family support and care network.
- Creates peace of mind.
- Ensures personal and medical wishes.
- Saves thousands of family dollars.
- Reduces employee absenteeism and work productivity issues due to family care situations.
- Avoids family conflicts and guilt issues over personal affairs.

"The Family Care Organizer" isn't a replacement for estate planning or Wills," states Wendell Moore, CPA and financial planner. "It's a resource that helps you identify and answer the "must have information" that individuals and families essentially need to help them through difficult and critical times. It ensures your wishes and financial intent."

"The Family Care Organizer" becomes your family's complete repository of information. It reveals the location of important papers and documents. It identifies family members having access to confidential information and keys. It organizes medical, legal, financial and insurance information. It helps you build both a professional and family support network.

"The Family Care Organizer" isn't about wealth," says Carl Beach, Executive. "It doesn't ask how much you have or what you're worth. It protects your financial privacy."

"The Family Care Organizer" enables you to plan, organize and communicate total family information, including last wishes. In time of crisis, it's invaluable in helping family members access care and honor personal requests. It saves families both time and money. It reduces family stress and potential guilt issues. It lessens the amount of work time family members have to take off due to family care issues.

This can really help our family!

"The Family Care Organizer" puts answers to personal questions in one place, so family members don't have to go on a "scavenger hunt" to find everything. It lists financial and legal advisors, bank accounts, trusts and legal documents. It defines your investments and clarifies your intent.

"I've known a number of situations," states bank officer Ben Reache, "where family members have liquidated assets intended for long term growth because they weren't instructed otherwise. It's critically important to make known your financial intent."

Planning! Preparing! Organizing! Communicating! Ensuring wishes and decisions! Helping your family build a professional and family support network. That's what **"The Family Care Organizer"** is all about.

While comprehensive, **"The Family Care Organizer"** is meant to be completed over a period of time and updated periodically. It is important that you take the time to investigate and complete all sections, as applicable to your household.

Suggestions for completing the **"The Family Care Organizer"**:

Why Not ?..............

- Invite your household to review *The Organizer*
- Create an informal setting by serving refreshments
- Discuss the importance of establishing a family care and support network
- Encourage each family member to participate
- Assign family members categories that need investigation
- Suggest that family members work slowly and in short time periods
- Gather your household periodically to discuss and update the information
- Establish a comfortable time frame for completing *The Organizer*
- Leave *The Organizer* in a convenient location where it is accessible to all family members

---

"The Family Care Organizer" is the easiest and most accessible way to establish a family support network. Everything you need in order to respond is instantly available.

Informed families do make better care decisions and provide stronger support.

The Family Care Builder Series

The Family Care Builder Series

"The Family Care Video Series"

An integral part of *"The Family Care Builder Series"* is **"The Family Care Video Series"**.

"The Family Care Video Series" offers a wealth of practical information that many of us have had to learn from experience in caring for family members. This is a resource that should be available in every home, company, church and library.

"The Family Care Video Series" helps family members understand aging/care issues, cope with guilt and stress, learn about care options, make informed decisions and access both community services and professionals.

Filmed nationally, and produced in beautifully styled question and answer segments, each tape of the three-tape set (length: approximately 30 minutes each) is designed to enable older adults to maintain independence and remain at home, assist care providers with care and service options and offer valuable resources about networking services and professionals.

NOTE: Employees receiving *"The Family Care Builder Series"* through your Human Resources Department, please check with your company library for viewing of **"The Family Care Video Series"**.

"The Family Care Video Series"

Tape 1: *"How to Care for Aging Parents and You"*
- Balancing competing responsibilities: family care, family, work and self.
- Helping older family members and parents maintain independence and quality of life.
- Understanding and expressing your emotions.
- Taking care of yourself: *working through family dynamics.*

Tape 2: *"How to Provide Care at Home"*
- Accessing home health care.
- Asking the right questions.
- Medicare's role in home care.
- Patient's rights and plan of care.
- Home care services, including Hospice.

Tape 3: *"How to Access Community Resources"*
- Identifying services.
- Examining payer sources.
- Building a support system.

- Family Resources
- The Majestic Grandeur of Housing Options
- The Fertile Plains of Community Resources
- The Vastness of Home Health Care
- Extended Care (Nursing Home)
- The Rugged Beauty of Estate Planning
- Community Services
- The Stunning Splendor of Long Term Care Insurance

Chapter 1
Choosing Your Itinerary

Choosing Your Itinerary

It's Chapter 1, so you're at the starting point. *"The beginning of what, you ask?"* The answer is a family care journey that will take you through forests, over mountains and even into the "Land of Oz". It's an extensive journey filled with side trips, guided tours and historical markers. **"The Family Care Roadmap"** meanders its way through so many family care questions, issues and concerns.

Like any trip, there are times when you'll move ahead very rapidly. But, there are also construction areas, detours and weather-related problems that slow your progress. Your family care journey will take time. It's meant to be taken over a period of days or weeks. It also directs you periodically to **"The Family Care Organizer"** and **"The Family Care Video Series"** at various stops along the journey.

Like any travel, it takes effort. However, you'll find it's been well worth it, when you've completed the trip. The information and awareness gained from your **"Roadmap"** travels will be of great benefit to you and your family. Though the material is both educational and serious in nature, we want you to have fun with your travels. Thus, we'll try our best to make your trip as enjoyable as possible.

The Price of Admission $$$$$

You ask, *"What if I don't want to make this commitment?"*   *"What if I don't want to pay the price of admission?"* These are good questions.

Tour Guide Response

If you don't take the time or make the effort to complete your family care journey, you'll leave some extremely important and very personal decisions to others. This of course, leads to a story........

Tour Guides Always Have Stories......

This one's humorous, but it also speaks volumes about "The Price of Admission."

It's a Story about Ism's   ⟶

The Ism's Story

Government Ism's:

- Socialism: If you have two cows, you give one to your neighbor.

- Communism: If you have two cows, you give both to the government, who gives you some milk.

- Fascism: If you have two cows, you keep the cows and give milk to the government. The government sells you the milk.

- Nazism: The government shoots you, drinks the milk and keeps the cows.

When it comes to family, letting others make your decisions can create similar "Ism's".

Family Ism's:

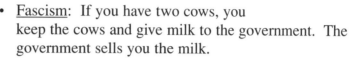

- Denialism: You want to keep both cows and drink the milk. But, you let the cows wander off and you never get around to milking.

- Realism: You're gone. "Heaven bound", of course. Down on earth, the government picks up your stray cows - keeps one, plus all rights to both cow's milk.

- Woeism: Your family members want the one cow. Government makes Solomonic decision. Sends second cow to processing plant. Family members each receive one steak, roast, rack of ribs and pound of ground chuck. Also, each receive pair of cowhide boots, but no milk. Government enjoys meal of milk fed veal, while retaining the first cow and all milk rights.

- Moralism: There is a moral to this "family-ism". You want to keep your cows? Create a herd? Develop a dairy? Then, build a corral. Brand your cows. Pasteurize your milk.

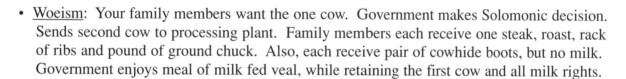

Truism

Do you prefer chocolate to skim milk? Malts to Maalox? Prime rib to burgers? It's all about choices and decisions; doing what's necessary to achieve the desired results. It's the same for you, as with the rest of your family. Because virtually every area of your life is impacted, making plans and implementing decisions becomes critical. Otherwise, rest assured that when the time comes, someone else will make them for you.

Underscoring The Importance Of "The Family Care" Journey

Moving Ahead

Let's turn from the humor of Ism's and cow issues to real life patterns and happenings.

Why should you take the time to read **"The Family Care Roadmap"**?
Why is completing **"The Family Care Organizer"** *so vitally important?*
Why is viewing **"The Family Care Video Series"** *so necessary?*

Let's look at the answer from three (3) perspectives:

Perspectives

1. Senior (55+)
2. Baby Boomer (35 - 60)
3. Emerging Life Patterns

The Senior (55+) Perspective

Regarding a lack of planning and preparedness, consider the following points from a recent AARP survey:

AARP SURVEY

- 54% of senior adults had done little or nothing to arrange for future housing needs.
- 37% of parent - child relationships had not talked about what would happen when they were older and needed help (family support).
- 36% of senior adults generally talked about family support, but made no plans.

Tragically

Only 14% of parent - child relationships had worked together to plan and prepare for the future. This included creating a family and professional support network, as well as putting into place disability planning documents, financial planning, medical directives and other legal documents.

Fear and Concerns

- 35% of senior adults expressed concerns about illnesses and failing health.
- 31% of senior adults expressed fear that they would not be able to care for themselves.
- 25% of senior adults expressed concern that they wouldn't have enough money to take care of themselves.

"Family Care From A Different Perspective"

The Baby Boomer's View

Regarding work place absenteeism and reduced job productivity, consider the key points taken from a recent USA Today (November 1998) article, entitled:

"Work Place Absenteeism Soars 25%: Costs Millions"

- Employers are losing millions of dollars as unscheduled family care absences reach their highest levels in 7 years, according to a survey of Human Resource Professionals.
- Dollars lost to absenteeism jumped 32% since last year.
- This loss represents nearly $4 million per company in the large company category.
- Family care issues are cited as the primary reason for employee absenteeism, instead of illness.
- Employee absenteeism jumped 25% since last year.
- Average cost of absenteeism to corporations rose from $572 per employee to as high as $757* in 1998 (*This figure does not include hiring temporary workers or over time payment to employees to cover absenteeism).
- Midsize firms were especially hit by absenteeism.

Guess What? Family Preparedness and Care Issues Will Increase

- We're an aging society burdened with longevity and care issues.
- Recent Medicare, insurance and government decisions place an increasing emphasis on family care and support.
- The estimated $10 trillion to be passed on to family members within the next decade underscores the growing importance of financial planning, investments and initiating trusts.
- The financial and emotional impact of families not being prepared for crisis, emergency and long term health concerns is tragically well-documented.

Did You Know?

90% of all families are not prepared either to respond or provide care and support in time of need, crisis, extended health concern or death. They lack information about policies, records, intent, personal wishes and how to create a family and professional support network.

From the "Gospel of Caregiving"

The DATA underscores the importance of

Planning
Organizing
Communicating

There's An Extra Family Care Ingredient

"It's called........

"Emerging Life Patterns"

RECIPE

- Couples now spend more time in an "empty nest" with each other, than they do in parenting.

- The average age of retirement is now 60. People who retire at 60 can expect to spend almost one-quarter of their lives beyond the primary wage-earning years.

- The average age of first marriage is as old as it's ever been.....and it's no longer uncommon for first children to be born to parents well into their thirties or beyond. It's also no longer uncommon to be paying college tuition as retirement is around the corner.

- Half of all marriages end in divorce.... And more older people are divorcing after long marriages.

- 80% of divorced people remarry. The resulting "blended" families hold the potential for more strain, more enriching relationships and more challenges for the later years.

- By 2010, about one-third of married couples with children will have a stepchild or an adopted child.

- Many women now spend more years caring for their aging parents than for their children.

- The average age of college students is rising.

- "Mid-Life" career changes are becoming common.

- More employers provide sabbaticals for study or travel.

- There are more four and even five generation families than ever before, with retirees in their 60's and 70's caring for parents in their 80's and 90's.

Americans are living longer than ever before. In fact, many feel this is the issue of this country - - - - "An aging society and how we adapt to a changing family structure never before seen in the history of the world."

NEXT...
"THE FAMILY
QUIZ SHOW"

Providing You Information About Your Trip Is......

"THE FAMILY QUIZ SHOW"

Sponsored in part by "Demographics" and "Aging Issues."

Announcer: "We're growing older..... But, that's OK. We should be proud of who we are, what we've accomplished and where we're going. At "THE FAMILY QUIZ SHOW", our concern is not that we're growing older..... but what changes this new longevity is presenting to us as individuals and families."

"OK contestants.......Answer the following:"

"True - False Family Quiz"

1. QUESTION: People aged 85+ make up the nation's fastest growing age group? True or False?

   ANSWER: *Believe it or not - True*

2. QUESTION: Approximately 58% of the 85+ age group still live in their own or in family member's homes? True or False?

   ANSWER: *False!! 78% is correct. Incredible!*

3. QUESTION: Families provide 40% of the care needed by older family members? True or False?

   ANSWER: *False!! 80% is more like it. Our later years usually bring frailty and some amount of dependence. Whatever our problems, we turn to our spouses and family members for help. Thus 80% of care needed by older family members is provided by the family.*

4. QUESTION: Increasingly, men are shouldering family care responsibilities? True or False?

   ANSWER: *True (It's progress, but please note that currently three-fourths of those caring for older loved ones are women.)*

"Bonus Round....Coming Up After This Commercial Break."

5. QUESTION: More than half of the women who provide care to older family members also work outside the home and nearly 40% are raising children? True or False?

   ANSWER: *True. These caretakers are referred to as the "sandwich generation," caught between caring for an aging parent while raising a child and working full time.*

6. QUESTION: The older population of this nation has not increased as rapidly as the rest of the population? True or False?

   ANSWER: *False. (If you missed this one, you were probably dozing or eating, as you skimmed past Question #1.) For your edification - the older population has increased far more rapidly than all other age groups.*

   If you are snacking at this point, take a moment as you consider the following numbers:

WOW!

- In the past two decades alone, the increase in the over 65 population was almost three times as great (56%) as that of the under 65 population (19%).
- The 75+ group is growing even faster than the 65-75 age group. The 85+ population is the fastest growing age group in America.

---

7. QUESTION: The majority of older persons relocate at retirement? True or False?

   ANSWER: *False - Contrary to popular myth and marketing, the majority of older persons do not relocate at retirement. They tend to either remain in the same neighborhood or within a few miles where they spent the years just prior to retirement.*

8. QUESTION: Most older adults end their days in a nursing home? True or False?

   ANSWER: *False - It's also a myth that most older adults end their days in a nursing home. It's more like 5%. Far more older Americans are staying in their own homes with safety modifications or taking advantage of home health care support and assisted living facilities. In all cases, they're maintaining at least some degree of independence due to increased availability of community based support services.*

Challenge Round
Next...

"Family Care Challenge Round"

The Quiz Ends

9. QUESTION: The 85+ age group has significantly lower discretionary spending levels than does the 65 - 75 age group? True or False?

   ANSWER: *True. The median CASH income of couples 85+ is approximately $12,000. This figure is significantly lower than the median cash income of couples aged 64 - 74 ($18,000).*

10. QUESTION: When asked to describe their ability to buy the food they needed, 18% of the 70+ age group responded, "I do not have enough money to buy the food I need," and 38% answered, "I usually have enough money to purchase the food I need." Only 37% responded, "I always have enough money to buy the food I need." True or False?

   ANSWER: *Tragically, it's true. In fact, 5% of the 70+ age group was without food for more than three days in a row the prior month. Approximately 28% had lost weight within the prior month, without trying. Almost 30% had no one to help them if they were sick in bed.*

Quiz Recap

It's pretty obvious that life as we know it is changing. What's happening impacts all ages of adults, but in particular both the seniors age group and the baby boomers.

These demographics, plus the other information presented in this chapter, underscore the importance of planning, organizing and communicating personal affairs. However independent we may be at any adult age, the plain and simple fact is that *"we are interdependent. We do need each other. We do need each other's support, love and care."*

"Communication is the Key!"

Did You Know?

- Over 80% of the elderly who live at or below the poverty level survive solely on Social Security and/or government entitlement programs.
- The elderly comprise the significant majority of homeowners in the U.S. Over 33% of persons 65+ owned their homes mortgage free as compared to approximately 12% of persons under age 65.

From the "Gospel of Caregiving"

"What Planning and Preparedness Mean to You..."

Planning, organizing, and communicating are more than acts of responsibility. They each represent one of the most caring and respectful gifts you can offer both to your family and extended family. *Each truly is an act of love*.

Family Priorities

- Make known medical and final wishes.
- Organize important financial, personal, legal, etc. documents.
- List your assets.
- Record your family's medical information.
- List key advisors.
- Detail location of bills and checks to be paid.
- Write instructions for bequeathing assets.
- Compile all household information.
- Put in writing all unsaid feelings and concerns.
- Read **"The Family Care Roadmap."***
- View **"The Caregiving Video Series."***
- Complete **"The Family Care Organizer."***

* **The Family Care Builder Series**

"Baseball?"

It's coming next!

"Choosing Your Family Care Itinerary" involves many choices and decisions.

Choosing...

The Baseball Game

I remember a homeplate umpire who was having a bad game. After another bad call on a pitch, the batter mumbled a few adjectives under his breath (colorful sailor language).

"What did you call me?" asked the angry umpire.

"Guess?" replied the batter. "You've guessed at everything else today."

Building a family care support network shouldn't be about guessing. It doesn't have to include poor care choices and decisions. Yet, as we look at our lives today - and those of our parents or adult children, we recognize that we often hesitate to reach out for support. We procrastinate and thus, don't plan. We let fear get in the way of family communication. We allow denial to roadblock our attempts to organize.

It Seems Like One More Thing To Do

Reading **"The Family Care Roadmap"** may seem like "one more thing to do." Completing **"The Family Care Organizer"** may seem like a task. Viewing **"The Family Care Videos"** may not be as exciting as watching television.

Please keep in mind that the information contained within these materials is highly important both to you and your loved ones. Just reflect for a moment regarding the benefits and value of this information:

Benefits

The Family Care Builder Series

- Creates peace of mind
- Ensures medical and personal wishes
- Plans, organizes and communicates your personal affairs
- Saves thousands of family dollars
- Lessens family stress, conflict and guilt issues
- Increases family communication
- Reduces employee absenteeism due to family care issues
- Enables families to make informed decisions about service and care options
- Builds a family and professional support system

CHOOSING AN ITINERARY

TOUR BUS

Next...

TOUR GUIDE SPECIAL

The Story of John Smith: Procrastinator

TOUR GUIDE
SPECIAL

"So, you've come to me to ask me about your future?" questioned the fortune teller. "Are you sure?.... really sure.... that you want to know?"

"Certainly," replied the ever-confident John Smith. After all, he was here only because of a Halloween challenge. Besides, he was a business executive, family man and civic leader. Surely, his future was as bright as his ever-radiant confidence.

The fortune-teller peered into her crystal ball. "You want a prediction about your future? Here's a glimpse of what will happen to you." "You're older," muttered the weathered and wrinkled forecaster of people's fates. "Your family is in conflict over both you and your affairs. You won't be able to live at home. Your personal decisions and medical wishes won't be honored. You'll begin to lose peace of mind, independence and soon, thousands of your dollars."

"Your fears will paralyze you," continued the soothsayer. "Your personal tragedies will be a direct result of your inability to make and carry out personal decisions." John sat there with a look of absolute shock, horror and dismay. "No way this is going to be my future!" he exclaimed. "You're just trying to frighten me. I'll do everything in my power to prevent these things from becoming reality!"

The fortune teller stared sadly at John. Quietly, she said *"Will you, John? Will you?"* Time passed. Slowly, the seeds of John's prediction began to creep into his life. Nourished by procrastination and denial, they began to take root and grow.

As John looked at himself and examined his responses regarding the future, he didn't realize how procrastination was affecting his ability to make decisions. He didn't see how doubt and worry limited his actions. He was blind to how his own denial clouded his thinking and justified his attitude.

"I know what needs to be done," John exclaimed. "I just haven't done it. What's the hurry about getting my personal affairs in order? Everything's all right today. There's no real sense of urgency when it comes to planning for the tomorrows of my life."

Guess what? Like a thief in the night, his lack of preparedness planning, organizing and communicating decisions and wishes, cruelly began to rob John of personal security. It shattered his peace of mind. It preyed on his weakness. It became his formula for personal tragedy.

In the end, John Smith's medical and personal wishes were not carried out. His finances became drained. His children were in frequent arguments and conflicts over his affairs. He lost any and all control over decisions. *He fell prey to procrastination.*

He didn't choose his family care itinerary.

Next...
"My Twilight
Zone"

Entering The Family Care Twilight Zone.....

<u>"A Real Life Story" (Mine)</u>

In my three decades of health and social services work, I've spent countless hours in hospital and home settings. I've personally witnessed via emergency and intensive care waiting rooms, both the chaos and dilemma of families encountering crisis, yet without any type of family preparedness planning and communication. I've seen many wrong decisions made during these intense moments involving personal, medical, legal and financial. I've shuddered as numerous care choices were poorly made; a direct result of little or no investigation of services.

Working with thousands of hospital patients and homebound clients in highly emotional and grief-related circumstances, I've seen adult children making decisions for parents without any knowledge or input as to their wishes. I've witnessed the financial drain of

> ### *Purpose*
>
> *"There is nothing in the world that helps an individual surmount his/her difficulties, survive disaster, remain healthy and happy, as the knowledge of a life task worthy of his/her devotion. You cannot advance in life with any joy, unless you are sure that where you are going has a destination and what you're doing has meaning. Purpose in life is the savior of life."*
>
> *From the "Gospel of Caregiving"*

thousands of family dollars, due in large part to family members not having proper legal, financial and health care documents / directives in place. I've watched as family members have gone on family scavenger hunts to locate and organize essential information.

In fact, it was this frantic search by family members that prompted my writing **"The Family Care Organizer"**. As the *Los Angeles Times* wrote, **"The Family Care Organizer"** puts all your family information, from health insurance to brokerage records, in one place so that your loved ones can respond in a time of need." (1997)

Choosing Your Family Care Itinerary

- Eliminates confusion and questions
- Diffuses "second guessing"
- Reduces "sibling squabbles"

If purpose is the "savior of life", then "taking charge of your life and decisions" is not far behind.

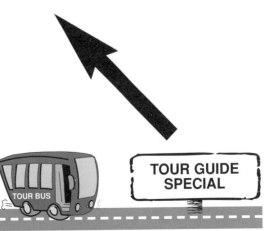

The Procrastination Plague

If you look around, you'll discover that there are many many John Smiths and hospital / home scenes as described. In fact, we're likely to be a part of this multitude.....affected by *The Procrastination Plague.*

When it comes to putting our personal affairs in order, the paralysis of "doing nothing" becomes our way of thinking. It handcuffs our decisions. Increasingly, we find it difficult to assume responsibility for organizing our individual or family information. We never seem to get around to making those extremely important personal, medical, legal and financial decisions.

> "Think this cannot happen to you? Guess again! It can and does occur everyday. As adults, age is not a factor."
>
> *From the "Gospel of Caregiving"*

If you're a senior adult, you're especially at risk. Your strongest desire may be to remain independent and live in your own home. Yet, you may soon discover that your children have made other arrangements. You may find yourself being moved into your son's or daughter's home or into a facility.

Most of us take a raincheck on our individual and family preparedness. Time passes. Our tomorrows come and go. We mortgage our future.

You think it's easy to create debt with credit cards? Look at how effortlessly it is for us to lose control of everything that's important to us, even our independence and homes.

We may say that we'll never let this happen to us, that we'll never leave our family hanging. But, we do. Why? It's primarily due to one overwhelming reason:

Procrastination

Procrastination stems from three basic causes:

1. <u>Self-doubt</u>: Being unsure of ourselves, we spend much time hesitating and second guessing.
2. <u>Frustration Tolerance</u>: We, by and large, don't want hassles. Our priority is being comfortable, rather than changing that to which we are accustomed.
3. <u>Lack of Ability to Handle Problem-Solving Skills</u>: In other words, we aren't able to handle challenges (even decisions) in our lives.

FEAR

FEAR Also Blocks Planning

When dominated by fear, we lose. Our families lose. In fact, it may cause us to lose control of everything that's important to us. This may include our decisions, personal wishes, finances, independence and family support. Fear plays a major role in procrastination.

So, as you look within or as you hear a loved one say, "I know what needs to be done, I just don't do it", examine very carefully the role that both procrastination and fear play.

Or, if you carry the attitude of:

- "What's the hurry about getting my personal affairs in order?"
- "There's no real sense of urgency, when it comes to planning for the tomorrows of my life."

Then, I'd suggest that you take an honest look at your inner feelings. Are you a procrastinator? Does your attitude have its basis in procrastination? If so, is your procrastination rooted in self-doubt, frustration, tolerance, or your lack of ability to handle problem solving skills?

The Family Care Vaccine

A procrastinating attitude can be overcome by making "a commitment to change" - a slow but definite one. Your Family Care Vaccine is made up of the following parts:

- Set one definite, measurable goal and accomplish it before setting another.
- Start with simple basic tasks which can be completed.
- Be flexible with your time, but use available moments to accomplish set goals.

IMPORTANT

"No matter a person's age, doing and accomplishing are very important to personal development."

From the "Gospel of Caregiving"

"The Best Time to Start Recovering From Procrastination is Now!"

"Choosing your Itinerary" is proactive...It means understanding
family care issues and making informed decisions.

NOTES

Chapter 2
Making Reservations

Making Reservations.....
Great Idea!!

But, Where? Who's Going?

Let's start with the family. Families decide family care journeys. They decide who's going and all destinations.

"Setting the Stage"
(For Your Family Journey)

Family Situations:

Act I   *You've tried to reach your uncle by phone for several days. Finally, you called his next- door neighbor, who told you that your uncle was taken to the hospital by ambulance after a serious illness. You are your uncle's only living relative.*

Act II   *You recently took time off to visit your mother. Your father passed away over a year ago. Upon arrival, you were both shocked and dismayed at how "bad" your mom looked. She appeared to be "worn out". Plus she had lost so much weight. Your kitchen investigation revealed little food, either in the refrigerator or the pantry. Also, the house in general, needed a good cleaning.*

Act III   *You've just finished talking to your 74-year-old father. You were puzzled and concerned. He sounded depressed and confused, but when you asked if anything was wrong, he said "No". He wouldn't talk further about himself. Unfortunately he lives 900 miles away.*

Act IV   *You've just hung up. Your daughter, age 26, has been involved in a car wreck. Though not life threatening, she's going to be hospitalized for two weeks, and will need follow-up care in the home. Upon arrival, you realize that you know nothing about her insurance or financial affairs? Where's the location of policies, documents and records? Does she have a safety deposit box? What bills need to be paid and when? Who will you call for follow-up service?*

The examples are both real and numerous. As each illustrates, *there may or may not be a single dramatic moment* when your relationship with a family member shifts and you assume increased responsibility for his / her care. Your "Family Care Journey" will take many twists and turns. Your traveling companions will also change, based on the situation.

"Making Family Care Reservations"...

Your Probabilities Are High!

It's Not Like Rolling Dice. But, Your Probabilities of Being Involved in Family Care are **HIGH!**

"What are the Odds?"

"What are the real risks that you or family members will be involved in family care?"

Consider these Risk Statistics:

- 1 in 88 risk that you'll need Home Owners Insurance

- 1 in 47 chance of your having an auto accident

- 2 in 5 chance that you'll need long term care

Did You Know?

More than 60% of the U.S. population will need long term care at some point. This family care figure becomes much higher, when you factor into the equation such things as illness, surgeries and accidents. Keep in mind, also, that almost all long-term care begins at home with family members providing the care. As each of the "Family Situations" examples illustrates, there may not be a single dramatic moment when your relationship with a family member shifts and you assume responsibility for his / her care.

From the "Gospel of Caregiving"

To Ponder...

Remember, taking on increased family care responsibilities can be nothing more than checking on a family member more frequently than before, due to a change of circumstances.

However, the opposite may result. Your family care change may be as abrupt as a phone call in the middle of the night telling you that a family member's health has <u>dramatically</u> changed.

Regardless of how subtle or abrupt the change may be, each family care situation will raise some issues that you may not have considered until now.

Next...Family Care Special Presentation

Family Care Special Presentation

Featuring

BIG DILEMMA!!
BIGGER DILEMMA!!
BIGGEST DILEMMA!!

No, It's Not the Name of a Movie. However, it is a Key Feature in Family Care....The Big Dilemma of:

"Deciding When and How to Involve Yourself in a Loved One's Life"

Your Difficulty - It may be difficult (even very difficult) to admit that this person, upon whom you've depended on in the past, may have to depend on you in the future.

Their Difficulty - Your loved one (even a parent) may fear becoming a burden to you OR LOSING INDEPENDENCE.

Strategy - There are numerous advantages to becoming involved in family care and support before problems develop into crisis. This gives both you and your family time to familiarize yourselves with your loved one's needs and desires, as well as an opportunity to explore the resources that can be called upon. Most important, early involvement and planning may lengthen the amount of time during which the loved one can live independently.

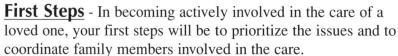

First Steps - In becoming actively involved in the care of a loved one, your first steps will be to prioritize the issues and to coordinate family members involved in the care.

"Currently 1 out 3 working Americans provides long term care to a family member. Average length of care is 10 hours weekly for nearly 6 years."

Next..."Family Talk"

32

"FAMILY TALK"

Words of Support and Care

A Family Care Tour "Must" Reservation

Ensuring quality care for a parent or older loved one, as well as periods of relief from care for family members depends in large part on family communication, cooperation and support. The special "Family Talk: Support and Care" section can be extremely beneficial in helping your family members both discuss and work through these issues surrounding care and support. This section becomes a wonderful tool for family discussion and an aid for clarifying concerns.

Here's The Menu
★ ★ ★ ★ Rated!

Appetizers:

    Family Talk #1:   Identifying Your Concerns and Issues
    Family Talk #2:   Sharing Concerns and Expressing Feelings

Salads:

    Family Talk #3:   Including Family Members
    Family Talk #4:   Anticipating Your Loved One's Emotional Reactions

Entrees:

    Family Talk #5:   Should Your Older Loved One Move in With You?
    Family Talk #6:   Recognize What Else is Happening

Dessert:

    Family Talk #7:   Care of Yourself as the Primary Care Provider

Suggestions

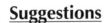

- Encourage family members to read and become familiar with the "Family Talk" section.
- Discuss family support and care issues, as they pertain to both current family care and future.
- Share feelings and concerns, regarding both your medical wishes and your role as a care provider.
- Define what care and support you feel you can comfortably provide.
- Create within your family a strong support network.
- Contact Professional assistance, as needed.
- View the Family Care Video **"How to Provide Care for Aging Parents and You"**.

FAMILY TALK #1

"Identifying Your Concerns and Issues"

Unless an emergency is involved, your first step is to gather more information and pinpoint where the problems lie. The question is, "What kind of information do you need?" Although specific information is essential, do not ignore your overall instincts and concerns. The following questions can be of value to you as you gather information:

Identifying Your Concerns and Issues

Social:

Does your loved one have:
- ongoing contact with other people on a regular basis?
- social life outside the family?

Physical Condition:

Does your loved one:
- have serious health problems?
- take medication?
- take medication without being reminded?
- have a disability that makes getting around difficult?

Self Care:

Is your loved one able to:
- do grocery shopping independently?
- prepare meals?
- bathe and dress independently?
- keep house clean and orderly?
- manage finances and insurance?
- avoid frequent accidents?

Emotional:

Does your loved one:
- become forgetful or confused about time and dates, etc?
- have frequent or unexpected mood changes for no apparent reason?
- complain about being bored and lonely?
- cry or seem sad a great deal of the time?

When you have specific details and can clearly outline the problems that have come to light, it will be important to share your concerns with your loved one and family members.

IDENTIFY

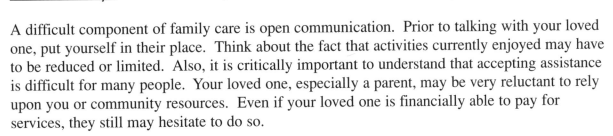

FAMILY TALK #2

"Sharing Concerns and Expressing Feelings"

Sounds Simple.....But Oftentimes,

It's Not Easy!

A difficult component of family care is open communication. Prior to talking with your loved one, put yourself in their place. Think about the fact that activities currently enjoyed may have to be reduced or limited. Also, it is critically important to understand that accepting assistance is difficult for many people. Your loved one, especially a parent, may be very reluctant to rely upon you or community resources. Even if your loved one is financially able to pay for services, they still may hesitate to do so.

Grief May Be Involved

If the person for whom you're providing care is older (parent, aunt, uncle, etc.), they may also be coping with a variety of grief-related situations - all at the same time. This includes the loss of a spouse or friends, decreasing abilities, physical discomfort and a loss of independence.

Also, added to the above, is the fact that they may feel lonely, isolated and frustrated as opportunities for social contacts and friendships diminish.

As all of these factors are added together, the person for whom you're providing care may not trust or share in your optimism, that even with his/her limitation, new opportunities are possible.

 In Grief.... The Glass is Often Seen as "Half Empty".

Later, As Acceptance and New Doors Open, The Glass May Be Seen as "Half Full".

As you share feelings and express concerns with your family members, listen intently. As part of *your* caring, it's important that you empathize with their feelings and worries.

FAMILY TALK #3

Include and Involve Family Members

Smoke Signals

One of the most important resources of family care is obviously the family. This includes both the immediate family and extended family. It also means intergenerational support, when possible.

Open and honest discussion about what various family members can reasonably offer, in terms of care and support to your loved one, is encouraged. This includes time, direct caregiving or financial support. This family meeting is an important method not only of building a strong family care and support network, but also of decreasing the burden of care on only one family member plus avoiding feelings of resentment and ill will later on.

Family Pow-Wow

At your family council, you might want to consider the following:

- Ask family members if they have noticed anything about your loved one that has caused them concern.
- Ask for suggestions or ideas on solutions to any identified problems.
- Decide what family resources can be called upon and divide up tasks and responsibilities among family members.
- Plan to contact family members who live far away. Ask for their suggestions and explore ways they can contribute toward the care.
- Agree that one person will be the family liaison, assuring a single focal point for communication with doctors or other professionals involved in the care.
- Write down your agreed-upon plan and distribute to all family members.
- Set dates to meet again to evaluate how well the plan is working.

After you have discussed the issues with your family and identified the problems you want to tackle, your family members will have a general idea of the kind of short-term assistance your loved one needs to continue living independently or functioning at an optimal level.

NOTE: Now would be an ideal time to watch the "Family Care" video **"How to Provide Care for Aging Parents and You"** (if you haven't reviewed it, as yet).

36

FAMILY TALK #4

Anticipating Your Loved One's Emotional Reactions

Storytime:

It was a tradition of the church for Elders each Sunday to serve communion to members who were homebound or hospitalized. In one case, an Elder walked into a hospital room to visit a 52-year-old man. The Elder entered with a greeting, identified himself and asked if the patient wanted (or was able) to receive communion. Unexpectedly, the man reached for a glass on the bedside table. Violently, he threw the glass against the wall. It shattered into a thousand pieces. Then he picked up a nearby tray. In one motion the contents on the tray were scattered across the floor. "Is this your answer?" he screamed. "I don't want you in here. GET OUT! Leave me alone!"

The Elder left the room. Devastated. Shattered. He didn't know what to do or what to think. He took what had happened very personally.

CLUE:

The Missing Piece

What the Elder didn't know upon entering the room, was that on the prior evening, the man learned he had cancer. It was malignant, spreading and critically serious. During the night in his aloneness, he'd had time to think and reflect. The impact of what was happening was beginning to soak through his numbness and shock. He was angry. He was furious. He was grieving. It really didn't matter who would have walked into his room. The same results would have happened. Shattered glass. Scattered dinner tray. Angry man.

Bottom Line:

In providing care and support to family members, especially older loved ones (even parents), it is essential that both you and your family care providers take time to review and to understand the various stages of grief and related "emotional reactions".

The Elder had not received training about grief issues and anticipating emotional reactions to grief responses. He didn't understand what was happening or know how to handle it.

FAMILY CARE TOUR OPTION   TOUR BUS   RESERVATIONS REQUIRED

"Moral To The Story"

Grief has responses.....
        And.......there are emotional reactions you can anticipate.....

The hospital patient was grieving. There was nothing personal directed toward the Elder. The outburst was an emotional reaction to a devastating psychological concern.

The patient, in every sense, was beginning the process of working through, understanding and reacting to his grief. Anger is a strong element when grief is involved.

In essence, the hospital scene would have happened. Instead of the Elder, it could have been a nurse who walked through the door. Maybe his wife. The grief reaction would have occurred. What might have been different was how the visitor understood and reacted to the patient's outbursts.

Grief
"Grief is usually difficult for an older person because of the difficulty of finding any kind of substitution for loss."

You Can Anticipate Your Loved One's Emotional Responses

There are emotional responses you can anticipate, even predict. These responses are linked not only to health concerns, but also to aging, divorce, job loss, moving and death in the family. These grief responses affect all ages. They include:

1. **Shock** - Our denial; we become temporarily anesthetized against the reality of the event.

2. **Emotional Release** - Our dreadful loss is realized.

3. **Utter Depression, Anxiety, Loneliness and Sense of Isolation** - We experience the depths of despair and hopelessness. Loneliness is believed to be the most difficult problem in old age.

Important: Remember that one source of these reactions may be the considerable amount of new learning that older persons undergo as they adapt to continual changes in their bodies, feelings and environment.

4. **Physical Symptoms of Distress** - Health-related problems, including eating and sleeping disorders may be experienced.

MORE.....
Emotional Responses You Can Anticipate...Even Predict...

5. <u>Panic</u> - We become unable to concentrate on anything other than our loss. We fear losing our minds. There may also be a sense of helplessness. These feelings are especially common among older men and women who once held positions of power and influence.

6. <u>Guilt</u> - We express regret and often blame others for our feelings. Life review is common for persons age 50+. In reviewing their lives, many older persons experience strong feelings of guilt, which means *"feeling ashamed."* Personal forgiveness for past events, happenings and circumstances is difficult for some individuals to accept.

7. <u>Hostility</u> - A sign that depression is lifting. Care providers need to be aware of this stage and not take it personally. This response may be a directly-linked response to a decline in physical health and the inevitability of death. Feelings of anger and rage are common among older persons.

Rage

Rage occurs when anger is suppressed over a long period of time. It is a furious, uncontrolled anger. It can evidence itself in violent anger, such as speech. Or, it can be physically violent.

Helping your loved one express anger and emotions is encouraged. It can be of great benefit in the emotional healing process.

Be aware that feelings of anger and rage may also be due to the neglect shown by society to an older person who is no longer economically productive.

8. <u>Inability to Return to Normal Activities</u> - We become more comfortable and familiar with our grief. Performing usual daily activities takes longer, if performed at all.

9. <u>Glimpse of Hope</u> - Emotional balance begins to return with proper support and encouragement.

10. <u>Acceptance</u> - We adjust our lives to reality. We are different than before. But, it is possible to live, love and laugh again.

Next . . .
"How Reminiscing Helps"

TOUR BUS

A FAMILY CARE
TOUR SPECIAL

Reminiscing's Role.......Or,

There's Value..........
In "Them Thar' Tales"

Before beginning *Family Talk #5,* please read and discuss this page on "Reminiscing". This important section has been included because of its value when caring for older loved ones with grief issues.

That Story's More Important Than You Think

Reminiscing is a key element when providing care and support for an older loved one. Again, this may include parents, siblings, relatives, and friends. Yet, a lot of folks do not understand the importance of reminiscing to the older individual.

We Overreact

I've heard this story before! Oftentimes, we overreact to hearing an older person's story for the millionth time. We need to get past this. We need to understand that when a person has difficulty looking forward or making plans and identifying with the future, they turn to the past. They do this as a "grief substitution" and as a coping skill.

Importance of Reminiscing to the Older Person:

Those were the days!

- Helps to maintain self-esteem and reinforces a sense of identity.
- Provides a sense of achievement and pleasure.
- Gains status by revealing selected elements of his/her life history.
- Strengthens coping skills related to the aging process.
- Places past experiences in perspective.
- Releases emotions such as grief.
- Establishes a common ground for communication.

Importance of Reminiscing to the Listener:

- Helps with knowledge and understanding about older persons and their time period.
- Builds a bridge between past experiences and the present.
- Establishes a mutually satisfying relationship through sharing of information and experiences.
- Provides an insight for gaining cues about the person's behavior in the present.

Tips:

- Take Time to Listen
- Ask Questions
- Give Your Loved One Time to Reflect
- Encourage Them to Write or Tape a Family History

- Show an Interest
- Express Feelings

"Reminiscing is a way of reliving, re-experiencing or savoring events of the past...that are personally significant."

FAMILY TALK #5

"Should Your Older Loved One Live With You?"

When providing care to an older loved one (including parents), the question might arise regarding "Should Your Older Love One Live With You?"

To assist you in this answer, please keep in mind that there are two levels of thought that should be considered.

1. **Personal** - This includes both your loved one as well as the family, whose home may become the new residence.

2. **Care and Services Options** - This involves determining what community services and professionals are available in your area.

A CONSIDERATION: "Should Your Older Loved One Live With You?"

1. Advantages:
    a. Combined expenses.
    b. Companionship for your loved one.
    c. Household tasks are combined under one roof.
    d. Peace of mind knowing your loved one is safe and secure.

2. Disadvantages:
    a. Tension having a loved one live with you.
    b. Compromised privacy.
    c. Your loved one's lifestyle and needs may conflict with your own.
    d. Your loved one may feel restricted in the new surroundings.

3. In making this important decision, you'll want to consider the following:

    • How do you feel your own life is going? Are you under stress from work, your marriage, financial difficulties or family problems? How is your health? Your spouse's?
    • What effect will this have on your relationship with others? For example, how do your spouse and your children feel about the possibility?

FAMILY TOUR
OPTIONS
RESERVATIONS
REQUIRED

The Questions Continue....
"Should Your Older Loved One Live With You?"

- Can your home accommodate another adult? Will your older loved one have a separate bedroom?

- Is your home safe and accessible for your older family member? Does your loved one have a handicap, which will necessitate physical changes in your house? Are there stairs your loved one will have to climb? Can he or she easily go outdoors, if this is desirable?

- What type of assistance will you have to provide now and in the future? Talk to your loved one's physician.

- If you are going to need assistance caring for your older loved one, is it available in your community? How much does it cost? Can you and your loved one afford to pay for it?

- If you work full time, who will care for your loved one when you are at your job?

- Is your immediate family prepared and willing to assist you? Specifically, what support are they prepared to give you?

- If you take the responsibility of becoming the primary family caregiver for your older loved one, can you expect to receive financial or other assistance from other family members?

- What impact will this have on your leisure time, vacations, time with friends, and social activities? How will you manage to preserve opportunities for these valuable experiences?

- Do you have a good relationship with your loved one? Does your spouse? Do your children?

- Do you have a backup plan in the event that you are unable to provide regular care for your loved one?

To a large extent, answers to these questions will guide you in making the decision to invite your older loved one to come and live with you.

VERY IMPORTANT

A cherished wish of most older individuals is to remain home and independent.

Oftentimes, this wish can be answered through home modifications and by utilizing home health care services.

Before making a decision to move a loved to your home or a facility, RESEARCH your options.

This will also prevent a lot of second guessing down the road and diffuse potential guilt issues.

NEXT...FAMILY TALK #6
RESERVATIONS
REQUIRED

"Like Snowflakes.......No Two Family Care Situations are Alike......"

FAMILY TALK #6

Recognize What Else is Happening!

Remember a key statement made earlier?

REMEMBER

"Being aware of grief responses to loss and change, helps family care providers both to understand the reactions of an older loved one and to clarify their own personal concerns.........."

Then we listed the major events and circumstances that trigger grief responses. The sources that dramatically affect the emotional well being of parents and older loved ones include:

- **Retirement**
- **Memory Lapses**

- **Life Review**
- **Decline in Health**

- **Loss of Independence**
- **Loss and Death**

Critical to remember is that through awareness of these concerns, family care providers can expect, even anticipate, emotional responses and reactions. This becomes a tremendously valuable tool in helping family members not only to share concerns, but also to work toward mutual solutions.

But, There's Also A

Next Stage.......

"We Adapt To Our Loss Or Change."

"Is This Important to Understand? YES! Because Sometimes You Have To Separate Care Needs From These Adaptive Behaviors."

THIS TRIGGERS "THE DOMINO EFFECT"

"The Domino Effect"

We adapt to our loss or change. This often comes out in our behavior. This is especially true with older loved ones, where adjusting to grief becomes more difficult.

Sometimes there's a fine line between our loved one's "care needs" and their "adaptive behaviors" to loss or change. Being able to distinguish the difference is very important as we determine our loved one's "real" issues, needs and concerns. This triggers what's necessary involving both family and professional care. This becomes "The Domino Effect".

ADAPTIVE BEHAVIORS TO LOSS OR CHANGE

Physical Complaints:
Some of these complaints have a real physical base. However, they may also be used by the older person as a way to gain a show of caring and attention that they may really need.

Denial:
Denying that changes are taking place may be an attempt to buy time until the person is ready to face the change.

Projection:
Often a first reaction to major loss is blaming something or someone else. This may be a means of dealing with the individual's own sense of guilt.

Paranoia:
There are legitimate fears to be faced by vulnerable, aged persons. Compounding this, there may be internal changes, such as hearing and vision loss, which augment fear and suspicion.

Rigidity or Stubbornness:
This may be an attempt to resist additional stress which we feel we cannot handle. It may be a way to retain control over our situation.

Selective Memory:
Remembering the happier times may be an avoidance of dwelling on the unpleasant reality of the present. Life review can also help resolve the longstanding conflicts of earlier life.

Regression:
May be a form of manipulative behavior to get needs fulfilled. Unresolved grief can also explain this behavior.

"Being Able to Distinguish Your Loved One's Real Issues and Needs, Triggers Appropriate Family and Professional Care."

"The Family Care Game Plan"

Instructions:

A. Call your family members into a huddle.
B. You're the "Family Care Quarterback".
C. You lead the discussion.

Game Plan for Your Loved One

1. Unless the situation presents an immediate danger to the individual's health and safety, give him/her time to reflect, think things over and adjust to the idea of accepting help. Let your loved one know that your support is available. Re-emphasize your offer to help find assistance at a later time.

2. If health and safety are at risk, communicate with your love one's physician(s). The path of least care resistance may come from following the physician's directive.

3. Establish the ground rules that most care options are "not set in concrete". Recommend trying a service for a limited period of time. If it works, stay with it. If not, then re-evaluate.

TOUCHDOWN

Oftentimes an older person will be receptive to this approach. They believe that this "assures your peace of mind." That's all right. The key point is that service and care options become initiated.

From the "Gospel of Caregiving"

4. In football, there are officials. They help "move the game along". In your "family care game plan", consider involving your loved one's clergy (if there is a relationship) and/or a trusted friend or neighbor. Both of these "officials" can help encourage and improve support to your game plan.

5. Remember, as much as possible, work out a care plan together. Older persons receiving care should have the opportunity to determine their own needs and pursue options that maximize independence.

FAMILY CARE GAME PLAN

"From Care of Others.......To Care of Yourself"

FAMILY TALK #7

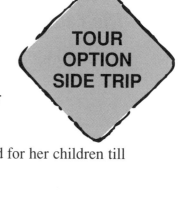

TOUR OPTION SIDE TRIP

- One out of three working Americans provides extended care to an older loved one.
- Average length of care is 10 hours weekly for nearly 6 years.
- A woman will spend more time caring for older loved ones than she did for her children till age 18.
- 80% of all care to older loved ones will be provided by the family.
- Only 5% of the elderly move to "nursing homes".

NEWSFLASH!!

What Does This Newsflash Mean?

As an aging society, family members (especially women) will actively play a major role in a loved one's care. This is NOT a "tomorrow" issue. Family care is real. If you do not take care of yourself as a care provider, the consequences can be severe. For example:

IMPACT ON	LEADS TO	CONSEQUENCES
Physical		Fatigue
Emotional		Stress
Social Participation		Withdrawal and Depression
Financial Status		Financial Drain
Living Arrangements		Conflict
Work Performance		Lost Productivity, Absenteeism
Family Lifestyle		Interrupted

It's Not Easy Taking Care of Yourself When You're "Caught in the Middle"

BONUS TOUR

This has created a "new term" for Care Providers..............

"The Sandwich Generation"

Definition:

The "Sandwich Generation" refers to care providers who try to balance:

- Caring for older loved ones
- Raising a family
- Working on a marriage
- Building a career
- Finding time for hobbies and personal fulfillment

It comes as NO Surprise.......but CARE DEMANDS on the "Sandwich Generation" are increasing. How time is balanced becomes crucial.

Did You Know?

- 95% of 40 year olds have at least one surviving parent.

- 80% of older persons eventually experience one or more chronic health problems.

- 33% of elderly persons have difficulties with personal care activities, such as bathing, dressing or eating.

- 25% of elderly persons have difficulties with home management activities, such as preparing meals, shopping, using the telephone and managing money.

From the "Gospel of Caregiving"

Woman...........

"The Traditional Caregiver"

Versus

"The Times....They are a Changing"

FAMILY CARE SIDE TRIP

Throughout history, women have been the family's "traditional care provider". This has not changed in today's world.

Change:

What <u>has changed</u> is the fact that more women are working. In fact, currently 63% of mothers are in the workplace. This creates a "real balancing problem" for "Sandwich Generation" women. Especially when you consider:

- The average woman spends 17 years of her life caring for children under age 18.

- The average woman spends nearly 20 years of her life caring for "dependent elderly" family members.

These multiple roles are creating "enormous pressure" for today's traditional caregiver. If this pressure persists for a long period of time, especially in cases where an older loved one has a serious impairment such as Alzheimer's disease, it can lead to depression and exhaustion on the caregiver's part.

It May Not Be Easy......But, You MUST Take Care of Yourself!

Next...

What Happens When You Don't Take Care of Yourself.

49

"For Whom the Bells Toll......."

They Tolled For My Mom (A True Story)

As an only child, my mother was very close to her mother. At age 83, her mother began to develop health problems. She grew frail. Home care and support became necessary.

Now, Let's Mix In Some Family Dynamics:

Her mother desired, even demanded that:
- My mom would provide the necessary care, as she wasn't working.
- She did not ever want to go to a nursing home.
- She would die, if she was moved into a nursing home.

Back to the Story

At first, the care represented only a few hours a day at her mother's house. But, over a period of time, her care needs increased.

Finally, mom moved her mother into our house. A hospital bed was also utilized to assist in the care. (Railings......up and down mattress adjustments.....grab bar).

Needing both help and time off, mother brought in home health assistance. This infuriated my grandmother. One by one, they were all chased off.

My mother remained the total careprovider. Trapped in her own house, it became like a prison. But mom had always catered to the needs, requests and demands of her mother. After all, she was an only child. She would also endure this.

Oh, I didn't tell you, but there was this bell. Whenever my grandmother needed something........You guessed it! She would ring the bell.

"The Ringing of the Bell.......
Became a Living Hell!"

Third Act: Scene II

My grandmother's care needs grew greater. My mom's own health began to decline. She was fatigued. Emotionally, she was exhausted.

Upon her doctor's recommendation, she finally made the decision to move her mother into a nursing home, so that 24 hour care could be provided. She had done all she could do, especially without help and support.

"As the Bell Rings"......Continues

"As The Bell Rings...."

"Like A True Soap Opera"

The Final Act

Like a true soap opera ending, my grandmother died in the nursing home. In fact, she died within two weeks. Did she die from spite or natural causes? It's hard to say. Her death was devastating to my mother. It wasn't so much that she died, but that her death occurred in a nursing home. Mom's guilt over this, almost destroyed her during the next couple of years.

The Humpty Disaster

"Remember Humpty Dumpty's Dilemma?" He fell off the wall and shattered into a 1,000 pieces. All the king's horses and all the king's men couldn't put Humpty together again.

My mom was shattered. Fortunately, through intensive counseling, a psychologist was able to help mother piece herself back together. It wasn't easy. It was a slow process. It was expensive.

Where were the Kids?

Mom's children (including me) lived close enough to help. However, during the time, mother didn't request or indicate that she needed help. As young adults, my siblings and I were somewhat naive about the whole thing. Plus, we were probably selfish, in that it was easier to look the other way.... to let someone else handle the care. There was never much discussion about what was transpiring. In the end, we provided little support or assistance.

Tragedy

The real tragedy was the fact that so much of this could have been avoided. There was virtually no communication, planning or preparing for my grandmother's care. Plus, her wishes were beyond reason. In this case, mom needed support.........from family members and professionals. She also needed to take care of herself. Both my grandmother and mother allowed years of "only child" scenarios, issues and concerns, to build and get in the way of a family care and support network. As her children, we took the "easy" road and "let" mom handle it. We didn't take the time to investigate or to really know what was happening. We had our own lives and families.

Have You Ever Been to an Opera?

If so, did you notice how long the final scene lasts? Invariably, a tragedy would befall the hero. He would keel over ......collapse ...... sing ....arise.........sing ....collapse again......sing and finally ascend. Mercifully, the curtain would come down.

Like the Last Scene of an Opera, when it comes to family care, there's a lot to keep in front of you. Not only about care and service options.....but also, about your role in this scenario. Certainly, not all family care cases are "terminal". However, like the opera scene, there are many peaks and valleys. Plus, it takes time for the scenario to unfold.

Epilogue

Most care providers find themselves in their situation suddenly and unexpectedly. Like my mom, they do the best they can, relying on experience, intuition and the advice of others. Unfortunately, for the average caregiver, this is not enough. Most care providers lack practical education on the physical, emotional and spiritual aspects of eldercare.

Impact of Care

If you do not balance your time, seek support and take care of yourself, caregiving can dramatically impact your:

- Physical and Emotional Health

- Social Participation

- Financial Status

- Living Arrangements

- Work Performance

- Family Lifestyle

> ### *Did You Know?*
> *Studies show that 36% of sandwich generation care providers don't know where to turn to find out about resources that might be useful, how to care for specific illnesses or even where they might find professional assistance.*
>
> *From the "Gospel of Caregiving"*

Next........"Feelings"

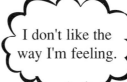

I don't like the way I'm feeling.

"Your Feelings May Change.......
As the Level of Your Love One's
Independence Changes"

Flashback:

Remember our previous thoughts about grief responses and emotional reactions? *They hit us just as hard as they impact our parents and older loved ones.*

As long as our loved ones (including parents) remain self reliant or independent, we may visit them quite often. Why? Love, obviously is one reason. But also, because we feel comfortable with them.

Or, we may only see them occasionally, because we know they're all right .... and we respect their independence.

However, if the amount of their independence should change, our relationship with them may also change.

As an illustration (check out the following box), if your older loved one shows signs of being less dependent, you may choose to see them more often in order to be there when they need you.

OR, you may become so frustrated and frightened by this change, that you do not feel you can face the situation. Your frequency of contact actually decreases. You may be unable to express openly your feelings.

Common Feelings: Adult Children to Older Loved Ones

Comfortable	Not Comfortable
Love	Anger-Hostility
Tenderness	Resentment
Generosity	Dread
Devotion	Helplessness-Shame
Concern	Guilt
Sadness	

↑ We Can Handle These (Touches our "Feelings")   ↑ Difficult for Us to Handle (Frustrates and Frightens Us)

53

Family Care Produces
"Feelings........"

(Not the song)
BUT,

Your Feelings as a Care Provider

It Happens

All families will most likely face a caregiving situation with regard to a family member. Your feelings, as you provide care may remain the same, or they may change dramatically.

Our Protectors

Remember the classic movie "El Cid" starring Charlton Heston? "El Cid" is Spain's mythological protector of the innocent. Strong and immortal, he is the hero both of the rich and the poor.

Throughout life, we may have looked upon our loved ones (especially parents and mentors) as strong, immortal and as our protectors. Even as adults, there remains within us, the hope, dream and/or wishes that they will still be there when we need them.

But, time passes........Life changes

What we hoped wouldn't happen, does happen. We begin to see ourselves as next in line. We feel more vulnerable.

We've talked........ about how grief intertwines itself within the lives of our older loved ones. It hits us too! As we look in the mirror and begin to witness our own vulnerability, we grieve. As a result, we may feel anger and sadness. We may be angry with our older loved one because they're growing old. Or, because they're abandoning us. In fact, we may show hostility and resentment toward those we love very dearly.

"A Bummer".......

We may dread further decline and responsibility. We may encounter feelings of shame (guilt) as we struggle with our own grief and sense of helplessness. In dealing with our guilt, we may overreact. "Role-reversal" is common, where we seemingly become the parent to our loved one. We not only take on care providing responsibilities, but we also become the sole decision maker. Our "over-reaction" may even lead us to totally dominate our loved ones.

"Words of Wisdom".......

In taking care of a loved one, it's wise to:

- Pay attention to your feelings as well as those of the person for whom you're caring.
- Set limits for yourself and what you can expect from others. A key question for yourself is "Can I handle this at this time?" In most cases, your answer will be "yes". There are times though, where you cannot and should not become the primary care provider to a loved one.
- Reach out for help by talking to family and friends; and even joining a support group.
- Accept the assistance that's available to meet the needs of an older loved one.

Bad News (Good News Comes Next)

When you walk into a family care situation blind, naive, without support or any previous planning and communicating, it can result in some serious consequences.

Impact on Your Health

Medical research indicates that if you are very stressed, you are more likely to become ill. You may develop ulcers, suffer from migraines or catch colds easily.

Some physicians believe that stress attacks the human immune system, leaving the body vulnerable to serious diseases, including cancer.

These same studies revealed that:
- 55% of care providers reported emotional strain;
- 37% of care providers reported visiting friends less often;
- 33% of care providers said they went out to dinner on fewer occasions;
- 50% of care providers reported having less time for themselves.

> **Care providers in the study were found to be more likely to use prescription drugs for depression, tension, and sleep disorders.**
>
> *From the "Gospel of Caregiving"*

Impact on Your Work Performance

Work related care provider problems included:
- 58% - Missed Work
- 48% - Work Interruptions
- 18% - Loss of Pay
- 17% - Regretted their Choice to Work
- 15% - Loss of Energy to do their Work Well
- 12% - Women quit jobs because of Caregiving Demands (5% men)

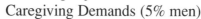

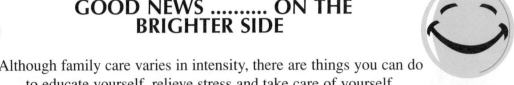

GOOD NEWS .... ON THE BRIGHTER SIDE

Although family care varies in intensity, there are things you can do to educate yourself, relieve stress and take care of yourself.

From the "Gospel of Caregiving":

"As a care provider, you must learn to take care of yourself or you'll be unable to function at home, work, etc."

NOTE: There's a Biblical passage that parallels this:

"In order to love others, you must first love yourself."

SELF CARE FOR THE CARE PROVIDER

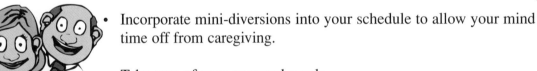

When providing extended care to a family member, why not:

• Combine two things that are highly positive for you - exercise and companionship.

• Allow time for rest - stick to a regular sleep schedule.

   • Incorporate mini-diversions into your schedule to allow your mind time off from caregiving.

   • Take care of your personal needs.

   • Become educated about services for your loved one in your home, or respite care for you (time off).

   • Join a support group for care providers.

   • Read materials on your loved one's disease or condition. Learn about physical and emotional changes.

• Ask for help; reach out to others; make joint family decisions as much as possible.

• Share your grief with family and friends (express your feelings).

"More Self Care Tips"........

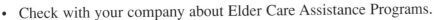

- Check with your company about Elder Care Assistance Programs.
- Seek professional support (professional therapist or pastoral counseling) to be your support.
- Spend time on simple pleasures.

  - Schedule time off just for yourself (It's not selfish! Take time for yourself).
  - Be patient with yourself and others (Be honest with yourself).
  - Maintain your sense of humor.
  - Look for signs of burnout.
  - Investigate local services.

Laughter is the best medicine

A Message to You

It's hard to fit self-care (you taking care of yourself) into crowded schedules. There are demands on your time. There are numerous responsibilities to juggle. **But do it, you must!**

Taking Care of You Means
- *Preparing*
- *Organizing*
- *Communicating*
- *And......Reaching Out!*

Tidbit:

"When asked, 80% of care-providing employees indicated they wanted more information about community resources, care and service options."

Only 3% of U.S. businesses have policies to assist employees caring for the elderly.

Now would be a great time to view the video "How to Provide Care for Aging Parents and You."

Leaving "Making Reservations"

TOUR BUS

Entering "Home Health Care"

"Please FastenYour Seatbelt...."
Your "Family Care" Journey
Is About to Begin!

All ABOARD Please!

Roadmap Policy

Like any trip, there can be detours and bumps in the road. The weather can be unpredictable. Your "Family Care" journey can help minimize these obstacles and steer your family in the right direction. We want your "Family Life" road to be smooth. It is our goal to help you arrive at your "Family Care" destination safely and quickly. HAVE A NICE TRIP!

• Family Resources

• The Majestic Grandeur of Housing Options

• The Fertile Plains of Community Resources

• The Vastness of Home Health Care

• Extended Care
(Nursing Home)

• The Rugged Beauty of Estate Planning

• Community Services

• The Stunning Splendor of
Long Term Care Insurance

The Trip Begins

Part III

The Vastness of Home Health Care

"Entering The Vastness Of Home Health Care"

PANORAMIC VIEW 100 YARDS AHEAD!

On most roadmaps there are recommended sights to see. Keeping in the same spirit, we have highlights to see as well, as we enter the "Vastness of Home Health Care".

Panoramic? Almost. The breadth of your view is really dependent on the size of your television screen. Highly recommended at this time is that you stop and view two tapes from **"The Family Care Video Series"**. This includes:

- *"How to Access Community Resources"*
- *"How to Provide Care at Home"*

These tapes will provide you with an outstanding overview about professional and community resources, as well as home health care. Both are approximately 25 minutes in length.

If bread and water are the staples of life, these subject areas are the key ingredients involving family care.

Filmed nationally and produced in question and answer format, these tapes take you on a panoramic journey involving both home health care and community resources.

An Olympic Hero: The Pentathlete

The video tape *"How to Access Community Resources"* is listed first for a very special reason. It introduces you to one of our real unsung heroes in life, "The Medical Social Worker". This special person plays a key role both in home health care and community resources.

From our vantage point, the Medical Social Worker is "Life's Pentathlete". In the Olympic Games, the Pentathlon requires an athlete to compete in five (5) different events. Obviously, this means these highly trained competitors have multiple skills and talents. To be the best, they have to master five difficult events.

This Also Describes "The Medical Social Worker.......... Life's Pentathlete"

60

O.K....O.K.. ."Why Are Medical Social Workers So Important?"

I've got a question!

Because, It's not easy for us to access community resources.

Let's face it. When it comes to identifying, accessing and understanding community resources, government entitlement programs and home health care, most of the time we're way out of our league. We're very much like tourists. We not only need a roadmap - we need a tour guide.

Case in Point

1. The traditional pattern of adult children taking care of older loved ones (including parents) is changing, as more people enter the work force. Because the number of people who work full time has vastly increased, families are now seeking new approaches to the problem of assuring satisfactory care.

2. Numerous services have been developed in recent years to help your older loved one remain independent and at home. But, even with the availability of this assistance, you and other family members often must juggle responsibilities of work, family and eldercare.

3. Services which support the needs of your older loved one exist in one form or another in nearly every community in America. Although there may be shortages of particular types of care, diverse resources can be tapped to help your loved one.

4. Nevertheless, it's often not easy to find out what specific supports are locally available, to understand payment options or to make decisions about what is the best care solution in particular circumstances.

The Difficulty in Accessing Community Resources has led to the Emerging Role of ....

"Life's Daily Hero..... The Medical Social Worker......"

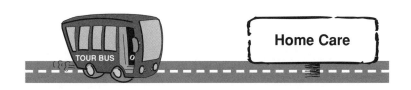

TOUR BUS

Home Care

Introducing A True Life Hero.....
"The Medical Social Worker"

Did You Know?

In the real Olympic games a Pentathlete's five competitions are
taken from among the following events:

Sprints	Shot Put	High Jump
Long Jump	Discus	Hurdle
Pole Vault	Distance Running	

Introducing the Five Events of the Medical Social Worker

If you substitute the word "role" for "event", you'll have a panoramic view of the Medical
Social Worker's five (5) highly specialized areas:

Event 1: Identify and connect you to needed services and resources including:
coordination of services, plus monitoring of in-home and nursing home
care.

Event 2: Assess your patient's condition, outline your care choices and develop a
plan of action.

Event 3: Teach you coping skills, including individual and family counseling.

Event 4: Help improve your patient's continuity of care.

Event 5: Evaluate finances, research payer options and recommend community
resources.

*Without a roadmap, it's easy for us to get lost. When family care is involved and you need help,
your tour guide is "The Medical Social Worker".*

Medical Social Workers may be contacted through home health care agencies, hospitals and the
yellow pages of your phone book.

Our Gold Medallist
- 80% of all care providers want more information about community resources.
- Most care providers don't know how to get to the "starting line" (where to start).
- Most care providers don't know how to "finish the race" (build a network of
services and support).
- *The Medical Social Worker provides you with specialized information about
service and care options.*

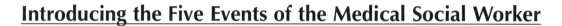

TOUR BUS

Historical
Marker

Historical Marker
On this spot in 1885 the first visiting nurse made a Home Visit

Historical Marker Ahead...

As your family care tour guide, the Medical Social Worker will personally guide you at some point into........

"The Vastness
of
HOME HEALTH CARE"....

Offering an umbrella of skilled and homemaker services, home health care agencies play a major role in the care of our loved ones at home. Stop for a moment and read this Historical Marker.

NURSE

Historical Marker
Home Health Care: Where the Past Meets the Future

"Be it known, that home health care is the oldest and most efficient form of healthcare. It is care provided by highly trained professionals using extremely high-tech equipment in the home. For years, it has been the preferred form of care, even for those who are terminally ill."

"Modern technology has developed to the point where virtually anything which is available in the hospital, can be provided at home. There is significant evidence that home care is less costly than other forms of care, and that it continues to be the most satisfying form of healthcare available to the general public. "Home care is the trend of the future."

Without question............Home health care will impact your future because of:
- New Technologies
- Cost Effectiveness
- Increasing Demand for Services

Home Care
Special Feature

Next...

"A Family Care Special Feature"
Home Health Care:

"Home Care is the Trend of the Future"

TWO THUMBS UP!!

★ ★ ★ ★ **Four Star Rated for Information**

The video "How To Provide Care at Home" is
definitely recommended to be reviewed at this time.

Key Growth Factors:

1. Care is delivered in the home:
   * We associate positive feelings with being at home.
   * If we're not feeling well, we want to be at home.
   * There is no more important social value than the home.
   * The home is particularly important in time of illness.

2. Home care promotes healing and reduces stress:
   * Unlike other forms of health care which can increase anxiety and stress, home care has the opposite effect.
   * Research indicates patients heal more quickly at home.

3. Care delivered in the home involves both the individual and the family:
   * The patient and family members are taught to participate in their health care.
   * Patients are taught how to get well and stay that way.
   * Home care serves to keep many seniors independent and at home.

4. Home care is personalized care:
   * The plan of care is tailored to the needs of each patient.
   * It allows a maximum amount of freedom for the individual.
   * Hospitals and nursing homes, by necessity, are a regimented and regulated environment.
   * Patients surrender a significant portion of their rights upon being admitted.

"WHEN IT COMES TO HOME HEALTH CARE...."

Our Tour's Just HIT The Tip of the ICEBERG

HOME HEALTH CARE SERVICES

SERVICE*	TYPE OF CARE PROVIDED
Nursing Care	• Offers skilled nursing care • Coordinates health care services • Teaches family members about caring for their loved one • Plans further patient care based on health assessment • Communicates with physicians regarding the patient's medical progress
Home Health Aide	• Can bathe and dress the patient • Helps patients with bathing and general hygiene • Often prepares meals and monitors the patient's nutrition
Occupational Therapist	• Provides therapy to help a patient with daily living activities • Can assess the patient's physical and mental limitations • Can assess the home environment for safety • Recommends changes in the environment and provides therapy in order to increase the patient's independence
Physical Therapist	• Provides therapy to help a patient regain mobility after a stroke, accident or impairing disability • Can teach the patient therapeutic exercises and show family care providers how to assist
Speech Therapist	• Provides therapy to help the patient regain or improve speech, reading and writing skills, comprehension and word production
Nutritionist	• Provides counseling services which may include meal preparation to accommodate diet restrictions

(* Medical Social Worker has been previously discussed)

"It's the small acts of kindness that greatly touch our lives."

65

HOME HEALTH CARE

POP QUIZ

(Didn't you just hate pop quizzes back in school? And the teachers always looked so happy.)

True or False? Home Health Care	Your Answer	
	True	False
1. Home Health Care is provided in a person's home to maintain or restore a patient's health and well-being?		
2. Home Health Care is a broad term referring to a range of assistance provided to persons at home who need help in meeting their needs?		
3. Skilled Care (nursing and therapies) is given under the general direction of a physician and consists of health services provided by licensed professionals?		
4. Support Services (non-skilled services) enable a person to live independently in the home. These services include assistance with personal needs, such as bathing and dressing; and chore services, which include shopping, meal preparation and light housekeeping?		
5. Home Health Care is provided through various private agencies, hospitals and public health departments?		
6. Expenses for skilled care are reimbursable through Medicare under specific conditions?		
7. Home Care referrals may be made by physicians, hospital staff, patients, community agencies, families, friends, and neighbors?		
8. Compared to hospitalization, home care services may reduce costs up to 90%?		

(Answers on next page)

THE VASTNESS OF HOME CARE!

I feel pretty confident

"Times up.........
So, How'd You Score?"

If you guessed **TRUE** on all questions, then you were absolutely right.

Just Remember:

Skilled Services	Payment Method
(Nursing and Therapies)	Medicare Medicaid Insurance Workman's Compensation Private Pay
Non-Skilled Services (Homemaking Services)	**Private Pay by the:** Individual, or Family Requesting Services; Unless Non-Skilled Services are linked to skilled services (paid by Medicare, etc. [top box]).

Home Health Care......

Services can be as simple as providing homemaking services, which allow an older adult to live independently; to providing advanced medical procedures, such as administering chemotherapy.

67

The Vastness of
HOME HEALTH CARE

Requirements for Medicare Coverage:

1. The required care includes part-time intermittent skilled nursing care, physical therapy or speech therapy.

2. The person is confined to home.

3. A doctor determines these services are needed and sets up the home health plan.

4. The home health agency providing the services participates in Medicare.

5. Care must be short term and for an acute rehabilitative condition.

Benefits of Medicare Home Health Coverage.......

• Medicare pays for the full approved cost of all covered home health visits.

• The home care agency providing service files the Medicare claim for coverage.

Covered Medicare Services

• Part-time or intermittent skilled nursing

• Physical and speech therapy

If any of the covered services are needed, Medicare can also pay for:

• Home Health Aide Services

• Occupational Therapy

• Medical Social Services

• Medical Supplies

• Durable medical equipment (80% of approved cost)

Next!
"A Bit of Magic"

Medicare Does Not Cover:

• Full-time nursing care

• Drugs and biologicals

• Meals delivered to the home

• Blood transfusions

THE VASTNESS OF HOME CARE!

offers you a Wealth of Information:

PRESTO! "Medicare In A Bottle"

MEDICARE

Medicare is a Health Insurance Program administered by the Government........
It provides hospital and Medical Insurance for people 65 years of age and older, as well as disabled individuals.

Consists of Two Parts:

1. Part A or Hospital Insurance helps pay for certain hospital, skilled nursing facility care and home health care.
2. Part B or Medical Insurance covers certain types of outpatient care, such as visits to a physician, laboratory fees and certain outpatient prescription drugs.

Brought To You By: The Health Care Financing Administration of the U.S. Department of Human Services........ Who, by the way, regularly publishes a Medicare Handbook.

Available at Your Nearby:

Social Security Offices (Cappuccino not included)

BAD NEWS - Medicare does not provide complete health care coverage. Gaps include deductibles, co-payments, limits on reimbursements for certain services, as well as lack of coverage for some services.

GOOD NEWS - You do not have to file a Medicare claim for covered services received from hospitals, skilled nursing homes, home health care agencies or hospices.

INSTRUCTIONS:
Take two
spoonfuls as
needed

SIDE EFFECTS:
(Just kidding!)

Next Stop
"Medicaid"

THE VASTNESS OF HOME CARE!

Skill? Or Luck?

Can You Perform the Same Magic for Medicaid?

MEDICAID

An assistance program that helps states provide health care services for needy and low income individuals. Many of these individuals also receive benefits from federal assistance programs.

Federal/State Program

The Federal government shares the cost of Medicaid services with the state. Federal funds contribute 50% to 75% of health care costs for eligible needy and low income individuals.

Eligibility

Each state sets its own eligibility requirements. If a person does not receive aid from a federal assistance program, Medicaid determines eligibility based on income and resources. The financial eligibility standards that govern Medicaid eligibility allow an individual, a couple or family to keep a small amount of income, plus certain resources. To establish income levels for Medicaid eligibility, the state sets an amount that it considers to be the minimum cost of the basic necessities of living.

Covered Services

Each state runs its own Medicaid program. Thus, covered services and eligibility requirements vary from state to state. Basic Medicaid health services that all states cover (at least partially) include:

- In-patient hospital services
- Physician services
- Family planning services
- Rural Health Clinic Services
- Home Health Services
- Hospice Services
- Outpatient hospital services
- Laboratory and X-Ray Services
- Medical and Surgical Services
- Medical & Surgical Services furnished by a Dentist
- Nursing Facility Services at Medicaid Certified Facility

INSTRUCTIONS:
Take two spoonfuls as needed

May be taken with Medicare (No kidding!)

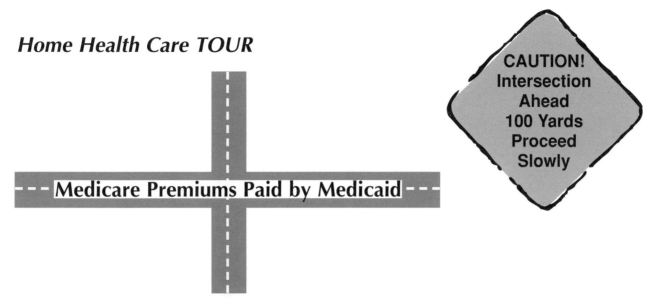

Home Health Care TOUR

Medicare Premiums Paid by Medicaid

CAUTION!
Intersection
Ahead
100 Yards
Proceed
Slowly

Please Read BEFORE Leaving This Intersection:

1. Medicaid pays the Medicare premiums, deductibles and coinsurance for certain low-income elderly and people with disabilities in the Medicare Part A - Hospital Insurance program and the Medicare Part B - Medical Insurance program.

2. This provision applies to individuals with incomes under 100% of the federal poverty line.

3. Medicaid also pays for premiums for Medicare Part B coverage for certain people whose incomes are between 100% and 120% of the federal poverty line.

4. In addition, Medicaid pays premiums for Medicare Part A coverage for certain working people with disabilities.

5. These are people who have incomes below 200% of the federal poverty line and limited resources, but whose income and resources render them ineligible for Medicaid.

Did You Know?

If family income is beneath Medicaid Standards, members of the family may be eligible for Medicaid benefits. Usually, resources such as a house, car and limited amounts of other property are not counted in determining resource levels.

When coverage for hospital or nursing home services is involved, staff at both facilities can assist you with completing necessary forms for providing proof of medical need or financial eligibility.

From the "Gospel of Caregiving"

"Fork in the Road"....

Not All Home Health Care Agencies Are The SAME

I've made reference to a fork in the road, because when it comes to selecting a Home Health Care Agency, not all agencies are the same. You'll want to do some research before making your decision about an agency.

Selecting A Home Health Care Agency

The fork is "symbolically" important. Why? Because not all agencies provide the same services or levels of care.

Why is this important to you?

1. Increasingly, home health care will play an important role in your family's care.

2. In most cases, you will have a choice of agencies under your healthcare plan.

It is highly recommended that you research and compare all home health care agencies available to your family or older loved one.

The Selection Process

Important Points to Consider:

- How long has the agency been in service?

- Is it licensed by the state and Medicare certified?

- Is service available 24 hours a day?

- Are professionals available - and not just by telephone?

- What specific range of service is provided?

- What are the charges for these services?

- Is Hospice part of the agency's service?

Here's What You Request:

The agency send information regarding

- Skilled and Support services

- Schedule of Charges

- Eligibility Requirements

72

"Compare Home Health Care Services"

IT'S IMPORTANT !!

Given a choice, you want the best care possible for your family members. If your insurance plan allows you a choice of home health care agencies, it's in your best interest to do some homework.

For example, most agencies have R.N's on staff. But, do their RN's have specialized nursing skills and training (see chart below)? If your patient needs wound care, does the agency have a wound/ostomy RN specialist? Many agencies have health care professionals with specialized training. If you have a choice of agencies, you want the highest quality of services. It is highly recommended that you do some research on the agencies. Use the following box and information on nursing and therapies as your guide.

Does The Agency Provide the Following Services?

Skilled Services:	Non-Skilled Support:	
Specialized Nursing	**Therapy**	**Home Support**
Wound/Ostomy	Physical	Housekeeping
IV Therapy	Speech	Personal Care
Mental Health	Occupational	
Cardio/Pulmonary		
Diabetes	Specialized	
Cancer	Registered Dietician	
AIDS	Medical Social Worker	
Pediatric		

"The more I believe in Angels, the more I see them all around me."

Home Health Care Professionals are like "Angels" when it comes to the care they provide.

Nursing

73

Introduces.......

The Home Care Nurse

- Works with the Physician to develop an individualized treatment plan for the patient.

- Responsible for providing skilled care in the home.

- Instructs both patient and family regarding the treatment plan.

Availability

- Short Term / Intermittent Care

- Extended Care

- Private Duty Care

- Around the Clock Services

Highly Skilled and Specialized

Includes:

1. **Enterostomal Therapy:**

   The Enterostomal therapy nurse teaches the patient and/or family in the selection and care of pouching systems and dressings used for colostomy, urinary diversion, draining wounds or fistula. Teaching the patient and family about the prevention and treatment of bedsores is also provided.

2. **Mental Health**

   A mental health nurse provides services to homebound patients. Under a doctor's or psychiatrist's orders, the mental health nurse focuses on counseling and special psychiatric interventions with the patient and his/her family.

3. **IV Therapy**

   IV Therapy is a specialized hi-tech care that allows a patient to receive medications, fluids or nutrition through the veins. Specially trained IV nurses provide care to the patient following the treatment plan ordered by the doctor. IV Therapy is frequently ordered in conjunction with general duty nursing or rehabilitative therapy services.

The Home Care Nurse

"Highly Skilled and Specialized"

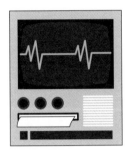

4. Cardio/Pulmonary Care

For the patient whose primary diagnosis is cardiac or respiratory related, the referring physician may specifically request cardio/pulmonary nursing care. In addition to attending to the medical needs of the patient, the cardio/pulmonary nurse concentrates on teaching the patient and family how to effectively manage and cope with the pulmonary or cardiac disease.

5. Cancer Care

Care is provided by nurses who have extensive knowledge of cancer treatment. Care involves pain management, including the signs and symptoms of infection, and monitoring the side effects of chemotherapy.

6. Diabetes Care

Care includes monitoring blood sugar levels, preparing insulin shots and teaching diabetics how to manage their own care. Instruction about daily foot care and use of a blood glucose monitor is also taught.

7. AIDS Care

The nurse helps the patient maintain a pain free level of comfort, stay involved in daily activities, assesses his/her condition for changes and monitors IV's used both for antibiotics and nutritional feedings.

8. Pediatric Care

a. Care includes monitoring a child or infant's heart and breathing problems.
b. Teaching families to administer and measure medications.
c. Providing instruction about dressing changes and infection control.
d. Teaching about specialized equipment and nutrition education.

Nursing

TOUR BUS

Next?
"The Therapists"

THE VASTNESS OF HOME CARE!

Physical

Occupational

Speech

"The Therapists"
(Sounds like a Western Movie Title)

Therapy services provide a wide variety of rehabilitation services to patients in the home care setting.

Acting on a physician's orders, a therapist conducts a comprehensive evaluation to determine the patient's present functional status and to develop an individualized plan of care.

WANTED By Families

The Physical Therapist Alias "The Instructor"

Description:
Physical Therapy may include gait training, teaching transfer techniques to care providers or developing an individualized exercise program.

A Physical Therapist's Instruction includes:

- Range of motion
- Bed mobility
- Transfer techniques
- Fitting of equipment
- Weight exercises
- Sitting balance
- Walking techniques
- Teaching of assistive devices

WANTED By Families

The Occupational Therapist Alias "The Assister"

Description:
The Occupational Therapist can:
- Teach personal care skills
- Teach use of assistive devices for daily living
- Assess a patient's ability to adapt and live independently at home
- Teach vocation / hobby skills
- Serve as a Home Safety Consultant

Services Bring Patients
GREAT REWARD

"The Occupational Therapist's..."

✔ HOME SAFETY CHECKLIST ✔

This checklist is to help you make your home safer. Use it to go through your home and look at the items that are listed below. If you check "No" on any items, your home is not as safe as it could be. By correcting items marked "No", you can improve your home safety and help prevent home accidents.

Home Safety Checklist	Yes	No
1. Are there sturdy handrails or banisters by all steps and stairs?	____	____
2. Is there adequate lighting for all stairs and hallways?	____	____
3. Is there a light switch at both the top and the bottom of stairs?	____	____
4. Are stairways and hallways clear of clutter and loose objects?	____	____
5. Is there a light switch by the doorway of each room?	____	____
6. Is there a flashlight, light switch or lamp beside your bed?	____	____
7. Are all electric cords placed close to walls, out of your pathway?	____	____
8. Are rugs secured around all edges?	____	____
9. Are rugs smooth and flat, with no folds or wrinkles?	____	____
10. Is there a list of emergency phone numbers by your phone? (Fire, Police, Emergency)	____	____
11. Are all medicines marked clearly? Name of medicine, date purchased, how taken, when taken?	____	____
12. Is there a non-skid surface on the floor of your bathtub or shower? (Non-skid strips or flowers, rubber mat?)	____	____
13. Are there adequate handholds for getting in and out of your bathtub?	____	____
14. Is there a long-handled sponge mop in your kitchen for cleaning up spills?	____	____
15. Are heat controls on your stove clearly marked and easy to read?	____	____

Occupational Therapists

Can Help You With:

HOME ACCIDENT PREVENTION

- Home accidents seldom "just happen" and many can be prevented.

- Falls are the most common cause of fatal injury in older people.

- Older people have more accidents due to poor eyesight and hearing.

- Arthritis, neurological diseases and balance problems are contributing factors to falls.

- Mishaps can also be the result of mental depression or poor physical condition.

- When accidents occur, older people are often severely injured and tend to heal slowly.

- A woman's bones can become thin and brittle with age, causing minor falls that result in broken hips.

- Many accidents can be prevented by improving safety habits:

GOOD IDEAS!

- Light all stairways. Put light switches at both the bottom and top of stairways.

- Use bedside remote-control light switches or night lights.

- Be sure stairways have sturdy handrails.

- Tack down carpeting on stairs and use non-skid treads.

- Remove throw rugs that tend to slide.

- Arrange furniture and other objects so they are not obstacles.

- Use "grab bars" on bathroom walls and non-skid mats or strips in the bathtub.

- Keep outdoor walkways and steps in good repair.

HEALTH

Personal health is also important in preventing falls. Because older people tend to become faint or dizzy when standing too quickly, experts recommend rising slowly from a sitting or lying position. Both illness and the side effects of medicine also increase the risk of falls.

"Also Wanted"
And.....
Not To Be Forgotten.........

(Especially in today's world of communication)

WANTED By Families

The Speech Therapist
Alias
"The Communicator"

Description:

- Teach Communication Skills

- Promote a Patient's Thinking Process

Additional Information:

Speech Therapy can improve work production, reading and writing skills, comprehension and use of augmentative communication skills.

"Services Bring Patients Great Reward"

MORE OF
THE VASTNESS
OF HOME CARE!
JUST AHEAD

HOME HEALTH CARE FEATURING "THE SKILLED SERVICES SUPPORTING CAST"

The Family Care Tour May Emphasize

"Home Care's Skilled Services"

 **STARRING**

Nurses
Therapists
Social Workers
Dieticians

 But, like every great movie, it's the supporting cast that pulls it all together...........In home care, it's....

"Non-Skilled Services"

Accepting the award on behalf of "Non-Skilled Services" is "Homemaking Services".

Homemaking Services Acceptance Speech:

 "As homemaking services, we're designed to provide such non-skilled services as:

- Light Housekeeping
- Laundry
- Grocery Shopping
- Personal Care
- Meal Preparation

There are even times, when we, as homemakers, may help with correspondence. You can contract our services through a home health care agency. Or, you may want to interview and hire us individually. WE ARE IMPORTANT! WE CAN MAKE both your patient's AND your family's life a lot easier."

"Thank you for your continuing support."

A Word to the Wise............

"Always make sure that you review your patient's Plan of Care and what you're paying for, before service begins."

↑   ↑   ↑

That's Great Advice!

?? The Question though.....is "What is the Plan of Care?"

THE PLAN OF CARE

- The doctor's plan of care is designed to give you as much coordinated professional support as possible.

- The plan of care describes your patient's condition, treatment and needs. It should be given in writing. You should not hesitate to ask questions if something is not clear.

Included in the Plan of Care should be information on:

1. What prescribed drugs are to be taken? Purpose and prescribed dosage, frequency and how taken?

2. What services are to be provided by Home Health Care? Frequency of visits, equipment needed and teaching of care to family members?

3. Special diets or nutrition restriction?

4. What activities can your patient do? What assistance is needed? Are there any precautions?

Essential

An essential part of any care plan is open communication between health care professionals and your family. This is especially important in updating your patient's condition and reviewing any changes that need to be made.

From the "Gospel of Caregiving"

"With Liberty and Justice for All......."

OR

From Our Home Care Tour Perspective.........

"What Are Your Rights?"

**UPON Discharge from a Hospital......
if Follow-up Home Care is Needed?**

Patient's Rights

Upon discharge from a hospital, a discharge planner must inform you of plans being made for the delivery of skilled services or equipment to your home and also give you a choice in the selection of services.

You are entitled to:

• Participate in the selection of services.

• Make informed decisions.

• Receive quality services outside the hospital.

• Refuse service.

Discharge Planning Is Patient Centered!

Upon leaving the hospital, you should understand all follow-up care needs and service options. You should be aware that you have been part of the decision making process.

**"A True Friend
Is The Greatest
Of All Blessings......"**

Many terms in life are familiar to us. We may have "heard" about Hospice. But, do we really understand and appreciate the essential role it plays in both a patient's and family's lives?

HOSPICE

What is Hospice?

Hospice is a form of home health care that provides emotional support and care for people in the final phase of a terminal illness, allowing them to live at home, as fully and comfortably as possible. Hospice doesn't hasten or postpone death. Rather, it affirms life and regards dying as a normal process.

What services does Hospice provide?

Hospice services include:

- Interdisciplinary team care: medical, nursing, pastoral, psychological, social work, home health aide, volunteer and consultant services;
- management of pain and other symptoms, as well as the performance of health care procedures ordered by the physician;
- instruction to family members in the care of the patient, including an explanation of the illness and preparation for what to expect as the illness progresses;
- emotional support and attention to the spiritual needs of both the patient and family;
- on-call services 24 hours-a-day; and
- service to the family during the time of bereavement.

What is the attending physician's role in Hospice?

The patient's attending physician is responsible for managing the patient's care. The Hospice nurse coordinates care with the attending physician.

"Affirming Life"............

What is the interdisciplinary team?

The Hospice interdisciplinary team consists of registered nurses, social workers, home health aides, a chaplain, volunteers, and a physician who works with the patient's attending physician. Efforts are coordinated to address patient and family needs most effectively, whether physical, psychosocial or spiritual.

What is the role of family in Hospice?

Family and friends are an important part of the Hospice program. They provide care and support to the patient. In turn, the Hospice team supports their efforts in every way possible.

Who pays for Hospice services?

Most Hospice services are covered by Medicare, Medicaid, health insurance or client payment. Limited community funds are available for families with no other way to pay for care, through non-profit Hospice agencies.

How are patients referred to Hospice?

Referrals may be made by physicians, hospital staff, churches, families, friends, neighbors, community agencies and patients themselves.

The Hospice Philosophy

There comes a time near the end of life when a person needs a special kind of care...a time when traditional treatments no longer offer the hope of a cure...a time when thoughts turn to dying with dignity and peace.

Hospice is that special kind of care.

Leaving
Home Care

TOUR BUS

Entering
Community
Resources

Part IV

The Fertile Plains of
Community Resources

Cruisin....

"The Fertile Plains of Community Resources"

This chapter bears this name, because of the abundance of service and care options available for families. (If you haven't done so as yet, now would be a great time to watch the video, **"How to Access Community Resources".**)

For Instance, our first Family Care Tour Stop takes us to

"The Check-Up That Changes Lives...."

Geriatric Assessment Centers

Commonly referred to as "a new type of doctor's appointment for the elderly."

Definition:

"Geriatric Assessments are performed at a center by a team of healthcare professionals, headed by a geriatrician. The specialist physician is specifically trained to help older people."

"A geriatric assessment is an evaluation, usually lasting 3 hours or more, into every aspect of a person's health."

Benefits of the Geriatric Assessment Approach:

- Helps patients live longer
- Helps patients stay out of hospitals and nursing homes
- Helps patients avoid unnecessary drugs
- Helps patients improve their diet and mood

The Team

- Geriatrician
- Registered Nurse
- Social Worker
- PLUS (on occasion) Dietician, Psychiatrist and Physical Therapist

Morsel

As many as half of assessments turn up previously undetected medical conditions.

"The Checkup That Changes Lives...."

Geriatric Assessments

The Physical

The geriatric team will do a physical, take a medical history and may also order screening tests. These tests are often overdue. For example, Seniors 75+ are least likely to be screened for cancer and thyroid problems, though these problems increase with age. Also, half of women over age 65 have never had a mammogram.

A Peek into "The Pill Box"

Believe It or Not:

- 70% of elderly Americans take more than one prescription drug daily; and
- 40% use at least one over the counter medication daily.

However, many of these drugs may be unnecessary and even dangerous.

The geriatric team will look carefully at all medications a person is taking. They will discontinue those that are no longer necessary and reduce the dosage of those that are. (Older people metabolize drugs more slowly and are more likely to experience side effects.) The geriatric team may also suggest that the family keep a notebook to record any drug side effects.

A Peek into "The Mind"

Suffering from Dementia:

- 1 in 10 people 65+ suffer from dementia
- 1 in 5 people 85+ suffer from dementia
- 1 in 5 elder persons have a psychiatric illness (usually depression or anxiety)

A geriatrician will test for these conditions as well as memory loss.

Dictionary

Dementia: "The gradual loss of mental acuity that used to be called senility." The good news is that some forms of dementia can be reversed. Depression can be treated with drugs. Mental confusion sometimes clears up when physical health improves.

From the "Gospel of Caregiving"

"An Older Person is Sick.....Because They're Sick; Not Because They're Old."

The Geriatric Care Plan

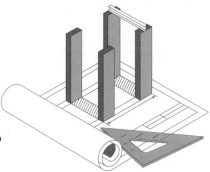

Family Conference

The geriatric team, in a final conference with the whole family, presents the medical findings and makes recommendations for the patient's care and housing. It is in this meeting, that a family's emotional and financial capacity to care for the elder person is considered.

The Payment

Geriatric assessment centers are usually located in large cities. Once you find a place to get assessed, you usually will pay little out of pocket.

Whether your older loved one gets the basic three hour evaluation ($100 - $300) or a complex assessment (requires additional time and testing), which costs as much as $1,800, usually up to 80% of this cost is covered by Medicare.

If your older loved one has supplemental insurance, the total cost could be substantially reduced.

When to Call a Geriatric Assessment Center?

A sudden decline in a parent's memory or mobility, or the prospect of nursing home placement are common prompters to set up an assessment.

But, the check-up can also be very useful when a family has nagging concerns about a parent - and isn't getting satisfactory answers from doctors.

For More Help

To find a hospital or medical center that offers comprehensive geriatric assessments, check out the following:

- Hospital - Internal Medicine, Family Practice, Psychiatry Staff
- Local Area Agency on Aging
- Your Family Physician
- V.A. Hospitals

.....Moving Forward

"The Answer, My Friend, is Blowing in the Wind......"

The singing group "Peter, Paul, and Mary" would be pleased. Today, "blowing in the wind" are community resources that provide answers regarding:

New Treatments for Old Ills

Here's a glimpse of what's happening:

	WHAT ARE THE FIRST SIGNS?	HOW IS IT TREATED?	HOW CAN IT BE PREVENTED?
Osteoarthritis *Affects virtually everyone over 60*	Aches and stiffness, especially in joints that have been injured in the past, generally decreasing or disappearing with rest. Sometimes it starts as a mild morning stiffness that eases each day after rising.	Over-the-counter pain relievers and anti-inflammatory drugs such as aspirin are often sufficient. Physical exercise can help restore joint mobility. Sometimes corticosteroid injections or surgery is necessary to repair or replace the damaged joint.	Avoid excessive joint stress, such as regular running on hard pavement. Build up muscle strength with exercise. Maintaining normal weight may help.
Vision Loss *In one form or another, affects almost every adult over 75*	Cataracts: blurring, double vision, and a general loss of visual acuity. Clouding of the lens is visible to others. Macular degeneration: blind spots in the middle of the visual field. Glaucoma: loss of peripheral vision. By this time the disease is already quite far along.	Cataract surgery clears the vision through removal of the clouded lens and replacement with an artificial one. There is no treatment for the most common kind of macular degeneration. The increased intraocular pressure that causes glaucoma can be relieved with drugs or surgery.	Sunglasses may be the simplest strategy for preventing cataracts and macular degeneration. Taking vitamins A and E may also help prevent cataracts. To detect glaucoma early, white adults over 60 and African American adults over 40 should have an eye exam every two years.
Hearing Loss *Affects about half of adults over 75*	Seeming unresponsiveness to conversation. Often it progresses to a state of social withdrawal because of frustration and embarrassment. Hearing impaired people may also be mistakenly seen as confused or uncooperative.	A hearing aid is usually the solution. But due largely to a perceived social stigma, only one in four of those who could benefit from wearing one are currently doing so. A hearing aid can actually slow the progression of deafness in some people.	Avoid exposure to loud noises. If hearing loss is suspected, seek treatment early since intervention can, in cases of infection, halt its progression. An observed link between hardening of the arteries and hearing loss suggests that a low-fat diet may help.

"New Treatments for Old Ills....."

	WHAT ARE THE FIRST SIGNS?	HOW IS IT TREATED?	HOW CAN IT BE PREVENTED?
Osteoporosis *Affects one in two women and one in three men over 75*	Sometimes low back pain. But osteoporosis often goes undiagnosed until a fall or other serious bone injury occurs, leading at times to a long convalescence and even death.	Osteoporosis is virtually impossible to reverse, but estrogen replacement therapy, weight-bearing exercise, and adequate dietary intake of calcium and Vitamin D can slow bone loss and reduce bone fractures.	Eat plenty of calcium during adolescence, but also later in life. Get plenty of weight bearing exercise but avoid athletic extremes or severe weight loss, which can decrease levels of bone-strengthening estrogen. With the onset of menopause, consider estrogen replacement therapy.
Diabetes *Affects one in 20 adults at 40; one in six adults aged 65 to 74*	Frequent urination, increased thirst, and repeated skin or urinary tract infections. Later symptoms include numbness in the legs or feet and blurred vision.	Eat foods low in fat, sugar, salt, and cholesterol; lose weight if appropriate; and exercise regularly. If you smoke, quit. If these strategies don't normalize blood sugar levels, you may need an oral blood sugar-lowering drug or injectable insulin.	Stay trim - weighing more than 20 percent above your ideal weight adds to your risk. Have annual eye exams and take care of your feet: Circulatory problems and nerve damage in diabetics increase the odds of feet infections that can necessitate amputation.
Stroke *Affects one in nine men and one in 14 women aged 65 to 69; one in six adults aged 75 to 79*	Sudden blurred vision, loss of vision in one eye, numbness or paralysis on one side of the body, difficulty speaking or understanding speech, loss of balance or coordination, or rapid onset of severe unexplained headache, confusion, or unusual behavior.	Clot-dissolving drugs reopen blocked arteries and minimize symptoms if given within a few hours after a stroke. If the stroke is caused by a ruptured vessel, blood pressure-lowering drugs and emergency surgery can help.	If your blood pressure is high, control it with diet, exercise or medication. Stop smoking. If you have heart rhythm abnormalities or a history of cardio-vascular disease, an aspirin a day can reduce your risk of the most common kind of stroke.
Alzheimer's Disease *Affects one in ten of those over 65 and nearly half of those over 85*	An inability to find the right words, especially nouns, making it difficult to distinguish from the normal memory loss of aging.	Tacrine recently became the first Alzheimer's drug approved by the Food and Drug Administration. But at best, it causes a modest improvement in memory and does not alter the illness's inevitable progression.	Unfortunately, there is no known way to prevent Alzheimer's. Some studies suggest that "active" minds, ever involved in learning new things, may be more resistant.

Chronic conditions take the greatest toll on adults over age 65 and those who care for them. This toll is starting to decline.......Thanks to the increasing availability of treatments.

When it comes to "Accessing Community Resources".....

The "Family Care Video Series" plays a major role.

What The Critics Say:

"The Caregiving Videos offer a wealth of practical information that many of us have had to learn from experience in caring for our parents in their last years. This is a resource that should be available in every community, either through local churches, agencies or resource centers."

Mary Nelson Keithahn
Church Educator Magazine

Community Services

The following pages offer a thumbnail sketch of community services, which are available in most metropolitan areas. Each of these services is highlighted in the video, **"How to Access Community Resources"**.

If you haven't done so, please stop at this time and watch **"How to Access Community Resources"**.

The Fertile Plains of Community Resources

Services reviewed in the video
"How to Access Community Resources":

Adult Day Care

Key Points:
1. Focus on Programs and Activities
2. Socialization
3. Daily Nutrition
4. Flexible Schedules
5. Caregiver Relief

Medical Day Care: Adult/Infants

Key Points:
1. Focus on Social Activities and Medical Care
2. Care to Chronically Ill/Disabled
3. Treatment by Nurses/Therapists
4. Medical Need
5. Doctor's Orders
6. Caregiver Relief

Stroke Survivor Support Groups

Key Points:
1. Rehabilitation is a Relearning Process
2. Support Helps Victims with Physical and Emotional Recovery
3. Teaches Care Providers How to Cope

Home Repairs

Key Points:
1. Research Company
2. Identify Repairs and Costs (Written)
3. Check References

There's So Much Helpful Information........
AND More To Come

⟶

More Community Resources

Dental Care

Key Points:
1. Impact of Neglect
2. Chronic Conditions
3. Preventive Care

Alternative Care Programs for Care Providers

Key Points:
1. 24 Hour Care in Hospital
2. Medical Care
3. Socialization
4. Doctor's Orders

Emergency Response Systems

Key Points:
1. Peace of Mind
2. Security
3. 24 Hour Services
4. Cost Effective

Arthritis Aquatic Program and Aqua-Ciser

Key Points:
1. Relieves Stiffness
2. Increases Endurance and Flexibility
3. Socialization
4. Cost Effective

Bathing Services

Key Points:
1. Personal Hygiene
2. Relaxing
3. Promotes Circulation
4. Relieves Stiffness
5. Promotes Self Esteem

Foot Care

Key Points:
1. Prevents Cuts which are Slow to Heal
2. Prevents Soreness/Irritation
3. Allows for Proper Fitting of Shoes
4. Important Services for Diabetics

"Last, But Not Least"

<u>Nutrition Services</u>

a. Home delivered meals
   - Designed for those who are homebound and cannot prepare their own meals.
   - Meals are delivered once/twice a day depending on the program.
   - Meals for those with special diets are available.
   - Fee: Sliding fee scale requiring payment on the basis of income or donation.

b. Congregate meal programs
   - Nutritious meals served in group settings.
   - Usually located in senior centers, local churches and school buildings.
   - Transportation is often available.
   - Fee: Usually donation basis.

For Help with
Community Resources Call:

- **Local Area Agency on Aging**

- **Church**

- **Senior Center**

- **United Way**

- **Medical Social Worker**

Leaving Community Resources

Entering Estate Planning

TOUR BUS

Part V

The Rugged Beauty of
Estate Planning

The Rugged Beauty of Estate Planning

New Destinations

Onward and Upward.......

Our "Family Care Roadmap" takes us on a new journey. OFF in the distance, we see a mountain range - "The Rugged Beauty of Estate Planning." Nearby, we see the following billboard.

ADVANCED PLANNING
"The single most important factor in building a family care network."

Neat sign......and without question we all agree that it's essential to provide as many facts as early as possible.

But,

That's easier said than done.

AN ESTATE PLANNING DILEMMA FOR FAMILIES

"The Art of COMMUNICATION"

One roadblock to any type of "Advanced Planning" is how to discuss planning and preparedness wishes and decisions.

Key Communication Issues
(From the Older Viewpoint)

1. As older adults, it's often difficult to face the reality that though our children have depended upon us in the past, that most likely in the future, we'll have to depend on them.

2. As older adults, we fear the possibility of becoming a burden on our children, or losing our freedom and independence.

3. As older adults, we find it difficult to discuss financial matters, especially money, due to its sensitive nature.

A Taxing Subject

Family discussions about money are often very taxing.   But, they don't have to be painful or avoided, if the underlying emotions are dealt with openly and honestly.

Family Care Journey

BONUS TOUR

Next

"Why Money is such a Sensitive Subject"

97

 **Money..... A Sensitive Subject**

The Family Care Survey Says:

Top 6 Answers Why Money is Such a Sensitive Subject:

1. We grow up as children depending on our parents for the necessities of life, things that money can buy.

2. Love and money often become synonymous in our young minds, a thinking which may continue forever.

3. During our transition from adolescence to adulthood our parents sometimes used money to express emotional support.

4. Thus, we grow up believing that money can express affection, encourage discipline, achieve closeness and other values.

5. We also learn that money can reveal sentiments of guilt, control or mistrust.

6. We realize very quickly (and it's reinforced daily) that money personifies our status in life - whether we've been "successful" or "made it".

Problem: Later in life as both parents and children mature, and it's time to begin discussions about Wills, estates and finances - so much of our childhood learning (love equals money) and other long concealed emotions often surface. Thus, money becomes a very sensitive subject. We let our money become symbolized with us. It becomes a discussion that's easy to avoid.

Result: While our avoidance of discussing finances, as well as other planning and preparedness issues may ease our short term uneasiness, it can also create major long term difficulties for families. This includes loss of decisions, personal finances, independence and home.

A Priority

"It's not a good idea for our parents or older loved ones to wait and plan a one-time discussion with adult children."

"Make it a priority to plan, organize and communicate all personal wishes and decisions. Fill in the picture little by little."

From the "Gospel of Caregiving"

The Family Financial Discussion

Discussions between parents and their adult children may also involve possible financial strategies that parents are considering. These strategies may be utilized as tax advantages or to solve existing money problems.

Financial Strategies: Options	Family Talk	
	Good Idea?	Not So Good?
1. Trading down to a smaller house or apartment. This move will reduce housing costs and free up some equity to invest toward future living expenses.		
2. Selling the house for tax advantages. Example: Taking advantage of an IRS rule that exempts from taxes as much as $125,000 in profit on the sale of a primary residence, if you are 55 or older.		
3. Taking out a reverse mortgage and receiving a loan in the form of a line of credit or monthly stipend. Your strategy may be choosing to receive payments based on your life expectancy, as the loan doesn't fall due until you move or die. At this point, the bank sells your house to pay the debt.		
4. Investigating a loan against the cash value of your life insurance. The strategy is that if you own a policy that has cash value, you can borrow against the cash value you've built up in the account. When you die, the loan plus interest, is deducted from the death benefit your beneficiaries receive.		

Parent - Adult Child Communications

Provide the opportunity to:
• Clarify each other's concerns and options.
• Identify special medical, social, and emotional concerns.
• Identify the range of resources available in your community.
• Identify housing options.
• Explore costs for Medical and Long Term Care.
• Affirm your support and willingness to help each other.
• Set parameters.
• Talk to professionals:
  - Financial   • Funeral Planning   • Physicians
  - Estate Planning   • Legal

Scenic View
Ahead

LOOK! THERE'S MT. ESTATE PLANNING!!

It's an important "Advanced Planning" landmark..... so obviously, you need to stop for a moment and take a look. (Our Family Care Roadmap offers so many unique sites and tidbits!)

Why is Estate Planning Important?

1. Estate Planning is a key component for families in building a family care network.

2. An Estate Plan provides you the opportunity to familiarize your family with your financial situation.

3. It covers Disability Planning as well as your last wishes.

4. It helps you put into place all legal, personal, medical and financial documents.

5. It allows you to direct how and to whom your property will be distributed after your death.

6. If you have no Estate Plan, your property could be distributed according to your state laws without regard to family needs or your desires.

7. There's also estate tax consideration. Currently, federal estate taxes range as high as 55%, significantly higher than federal income tax rates.

Who Needs Estate Planning?

ME?
You?
Our Parents?
Our Children?
Our Relatives?

ANSWER:

- *Anyone* who owns property, including:
- A home
- A car
- Bank account
- Investments
- Business interests
- Retirement plan
- Collectibles,
- Etc....

The Rugged Beauty of Estate Planning

"O.K.....Family Care Travelers
It's PERSONAL QUIZ TIME!"

"Check Yourself on Your Estate Planning"

Are you on track with your estate planning? What about your parents or adult children? Use the following ten-point checklist to find out. Just answer each question "yes" or "no". Does your estate plan:	YES	NO
1. Include an up-to-date Will?		
2. Name a guardian for your minor children?		
3. Name an executor (or personal representative) and trustee whom you are confident will carry out your wishes?		
4. Take into consideration any special medical or educational needs certain family members may have?		
5. Include provisions for long-term health care for you and your spouse and/or other dependents should the need arise?		
6. Take advantage of the benefits of lifetime gifts?		
7. Include charitable gifts?		
8. Provide investment assistance for family members who may need help managing their inheritances?		
9. Minimize taxes?		
10. Provide a smooth and tax-advantaged transfer of your business interests at your retirement or death, or if you become disabled?		

**Every "NO" Answer ......
May indicate a gap - not only in your retirement planning,
but also in your family support network.**

When To Review Your Estate Plan ?

> "Personal and family changes can make yesterday's well-devised estate plan wholly inadequate today. Consequently, you should be aware of events that may signal the need for an estate plan review and possible revision."

1. **Births:** You'll probably want to consider the needs of a new child or grandchild in planning your estate.

2. **Deaths:** The death of your spouse or another beneficiary can greatly affect your plan. So too, can the death of your executor, your children's guardian or your trustee.

3. **Marriages:** If you marry, you most certainly will want to review your estate plan. When your children marry, you may want to revise your plan.

4. **Divorces:** Most people review their estate plans if they divorce. But many fail to consider the effects of a beneficiary's divorce on that beneficiary's inheritance. As an example, suppose your Will gives your son and his wife joint ownership in your home. Think of the problems that could arise if they divorce and you don't revise your Will.

5. **Moves Out of State:** If you move to a new state, your estate will be settled according to the laws of that state. Certain provisions of your estate plan that are valid in your current state of residence could be invalid under the laws of the new state. Also, having your executor and witnesses to your Will residing in a state many miles away, could hamper the administration and settlement of your estate.

6. **Changes in Estate Composition:** A substantial increase or decrease in the value of your estate may throw your plan out of kilter and make a review or revision necessary.

7. **Business Changes:** Certain business changes signal time for an estate plan review. These changes include starting, buying or selling a business; entering into a buy-sell agreement that provides for the sale of your business when you die; changing your business's legal form; and the death of a business partner or another important member of your firm.

8. **Tax Law Changes:** On average, the tax law changes every couple of years. Any change in the law may make your estate plan outdated.

9. **Summary:** The best way to keep your estate plan up-to-date is to review it on a regular basis.

The Rugged Beauty of Estate Planning

Where There's a "Will"......
There's a Way

First Step to Planning Your Estate: Create A Will

A WILL IS A POWERFUL PLANNING TOOL

Through a properly drawn Will, you can:

- Protect your family by making provisions to meet their present and future financial needs.
- Minimize taxes that might reduce the size of your estate.
- Name an experienced executor or personal representative who will ensure that your wishes are carried out.
- Name a guardian for your minor children.
- Establish trusts to manage the inheritances of any beneficiaries who may be minors or are otherwise inexperienced in asset management.
- Make sure your assets will be managed prudently (by appointing a qualified trustee of a trust created in your Will, for example).
- Avoid the delays and the added expense that intestacy proceedings may involve.
- Secure the peace of mind of knowing your family and other heirs will be well taken care of according to your desires.

---

1. The first step to planning your estate is threefold:

   a. Be honest with yourself.
b. Recognize that for all members of your family, money represents feelings and emotions.
c. Work from a strategy.

2. A Will is a final statement of your wishes. It's your expression of love for your family and friends, made in financial terms. The provisions of your Will can help to protect a family. Or, they can cause unintended pain and strife.

3. Wills are also vitally important if you are single, divorced or widowed. If you die without a Will (intestate), your state's probate court will administer your estate. If you are single and childless, your assets will be distributed among your relatives. If you have no living relatives, your assets will revert to the state. In either case, partner, friends and charities you may hold dear will receive nothing.

Communicate Wishes

The Strategy
(Creating A Will)

Contemplating Your Moves

a. Set aside time to think through your Will.

b. Decide how you want your estate distributed.

c. Hold a meeting with your children to discuss your intentions.

d. Consider inviting a professional (i.e., attorney or financial planner) to the meeting.

e. Listen to your children's reactions.

f. Think over your family's responses.

g. Write your children a "letter from the heart" to be read at the same time of the Will.

h. Talk to professionals. If possible, involve your adult children, both as listeners and as support. (Professionals include: lawyers, physicians, financial planners, estate planners, funeral planners, etc.)

My next move?

> **From the *"Gospel of Caregiving"*:**
>
> Your awareness, thoughtfulness and willingness to discuss your intentions can make it easier for your children to understand and accept your final decisions.

i. Complete a list of your assets, income and debts, plus a listing of your policies and coverage.

j. Put one child (or children) on your checking/savings account and safe deposit box as an alternative signatory.

k. Make arrangements for emergencies before a real emergency arises.

l. Realize that with proper planning and preparedness, neither you nor your children will have to work through "forgiveness issues" for the tough choices you'll inevitably have to make. You'll have already made them.

ESTATE
PLANNING
More Than
A Game

"Checkmate!"

Once you've created a Will, the following information should be in place regarding:

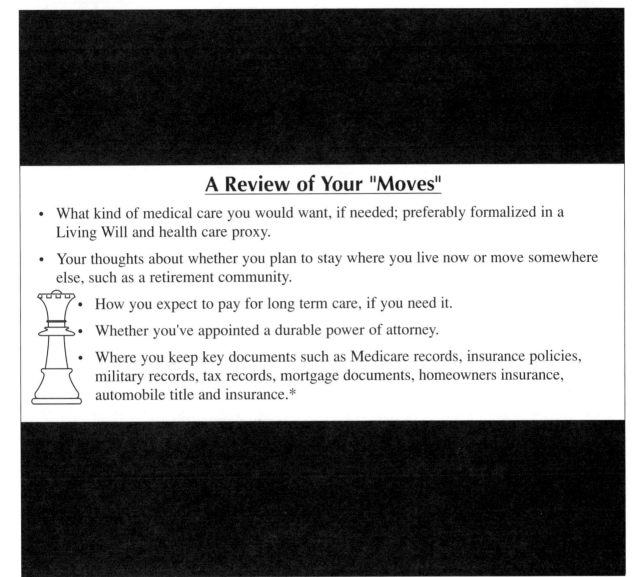

A Review of Your "Moves"

- What kind of medical care you would want, if needed; preferably formalized in a Living Will and health care proxy.

- Your thoughts about whether you plan to stay where you live now or move somewhere else, such as a retirement community.

- How you expect to pay for long term care, if you need it.

- Whether you've appointed a durable power of attorney.

- Where you keep key documents such as Medicare records, insurance policies, military records, tax records, mortgage documents, homeowners insurance, automobile title and insurance.*

* Note:

"The Family Care Organizer" will help you compile and list this information.

The Rugged Beauty of Estate Planning

THE CHOICE IS YOURS!

Choosing An Executor

An important estate planning decision is who to name as your executor or personal representative. This person will administer your estate and distribute your assets to beneficiaries as directed by your Will. You can choose almost anyone who is an adult and who is legally competent to serve as your Executor. This may include your spouse, siblings, friend, legal advisor, financial advisor, etc.

Duties of an Executor or Personal Representative

The terms executor and personal representative are interchangeable and vary from state to state. The duties and responsibilities, however are basically the same. An executor generally must:

- Collect and provide safekeeping for the estate's assets;

- Notify creditors and pay all valid debts;

- Collect any sums owed the estate;

- File claims for pension and profit-sharing plan benefits, Social Security benefits and veteran's benefits;

- Manage the estate's assets;

- Sell assets, as directed by a Will or required by state law, to pay estate expenses or legacies;

- Distribute assets to beneficiaries;

- File the decedent's final federal income-tax return;

- Choose a tax year for the estate;

- File the estate's income tax returns;

- File State death-tax returns;

- Complete and file the federal estate tax return.

Moving Ahead...

CAUTION!
Road under construction. Possible delays.

The Rugged Beauty of Estate Planning

INFORMATION AHEAD
Expect momentary delays.

As with any trip, delays are inevitable. On your "Family Care Roadmap" journey, this delay will be brief.....Just Long Enough to Stop (and examine)........

A KEY DOCUMENT

Durable Power of Attorney

A key document that both you and your loved ones need to have in place is a "Durable Power of Attorney". This legal document appoints someone to make financial decisions for you should you become ill or incompetent.

Either a "Standard Power of Attorney" or "Durable Power of Attorney" can be established to authorize a person to handle personal or financial matters for another.

Because the "Standard Power of Attorney" loses its effectiveness if you (the principal) become legally incompetent, a "Durable Power of Attorney" is usually recommended. It will continue in force if a person becomes incapacitated.

? ? ? ? ? ? ? ? ? ? ? ? ?

A Thought Provoking Question?

Who will manage your assets and make healthcare decisions for you if you become incapacitated and can no longer handle these responsibilities yourself? Unless you plan ahead, the answer is a guardian or conservator appointed by the state court.

? ? ? ? ? ? ? ? ? ? ? ? ?

Ladies and Gentleman..........Your tour is now entering into

"The Land of Disability Planning"

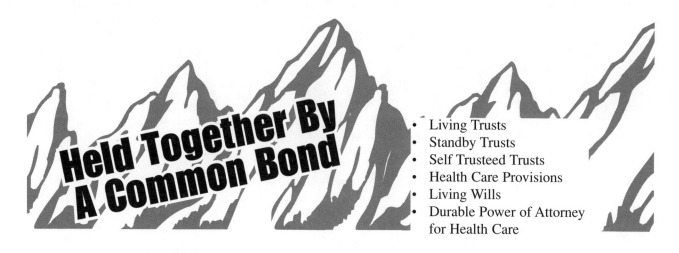

Held Together By A Common Bond

- Living Trusts
- Standby Trusts
- Self Trusteed Trusts
- Health Care Provisions
- Living Wills
- Durable Power of Attorney for Health Care

Into The Land of Disability Planning

Without question, we want to be in control of our decisions and choices. This includes appointing someone to manage our assets and make healthcare decisions if we become incapacitated.

This can be accomplished by utilizing the following strategies and options regarding "Disability Planning".

A. Living Trusts

1. What is the best strategy to avoid probate and protect your financial privacy?
   ANSWER: A Living Trust

2. What is a Living Trust? It is a legal agreement under which you transfer assets to the trust to be managed by a trustee for the benefit of one or more people, generally you and your spouse.

3. The trustee is responsible for administering the trust and managing all trust assets.

4. You can serve as your own trustee during your lifetime, or you may want to choose another person or organization to serve as your trustee. (Example: bank or trust company)

5. A Living Trust can hold all types of assets - including your investment portfolio, collectibles and your closely held business.

6. Unlike your Will, a Living Trust is not a matter of public record. If your trust agreement provides for your trust to continue after your death, the assets in the trust at your death will escape probate and any ensuing publicity.

7. Because a Living Trust must follow your explicit wishes, it must be established long before any concerns arise about your mental capability, so no questions can be raised about its intentions.

The Living Trust Tour Continues...

Living Trusts (continued)

8. Living Trusts also provide a clear track record of your financial activity. Your trustee is required by law to follow your wishes concerning how the fund is invested and to keep records of all funds held, invested or distributed by the trust. This protects you, family members and any future beneficiaries of the trust from suggestions of misuse.

9. The Living Trust can be changed as long as you are competent.

10. A Living Trust does not qualify you for Medicaid.

11. Although state laws vary, anyone with real estate or a net worth of at least $60,000 can use a Living Trust to avoid probate.

B. Standby Trusts.......A Disability Planning Option

1. If you prefer to manage your assets yourself, a "standby trust" may be the right "Disability Planning Tool".

2. In this trust, your trustee takes over management of your assets only if a predetermined event, such as your incapacity occurs.

3. You may reassume management of your assets if and when you recover from your incapacity.

REMEMBER

You have choices when it comes to planning your affairs. It takes time and research to determine what's best for you.

From the "Gospel of Caregiving"

"Advanced Planning" is the key to this kingdom.

"Off in the Distance..."

"You see Additional Disability Planning Ranges."

C. <u>Self Trusteed Trusts</u>

1. An alternative "Disability Planning Tool" is for you to serve as trustee of your Living Trust, making sure you've named a successor trustee to take over management of your assets while you're incapacitated.

2. Your assets will continue to be managed according to your wishes with no interruption.

D. <u>Health Care Provisions</u>

1. It is highly recommended to include disability and long term care insurance in your "Advanced Planning" to help preserve assets. These will be featured tour stops later in our "Family Care Roadmap" journey.

2. A "Living Will" or "durable power of attorney for health care" helps ensure that wishes are carried out if you are unable to make health care decisions yourself. A "Living Will" is examined on the next page.

For Your Information

All 50 states now recognize the rights of terminally ill patients to "refuse life - prolonging treatment." But, in the confusion and trauma of an illness, these rights and the patient's wishes can be ignored. Family members not ready to say goodbye, doctors who see their mission as preserving life at all costs, hospitals worried about litigation, all may undermine the law and drown out the lone voice of the patient. Unfortunately, there is no guaranteed way to avoid the nightmare scenario. However, you and your loved ones can greatly increase the chances that wishes will be respected, if you plan ahead and keep in frequent communication with doctors.

How to Make Them Work

E. Living Wills

Definition: *"Living Will"*

A "Living Will" speaks for you when you're unable to do so. Usually the purpose of a "Living Will" is to express your desire not to receive extraordinary medical treatment.

- You determine the kind of medical care you want under the circumstances you describe.

- You should express your wishes in as much detail as possible, so that medical care providers will be able to understand your intent clearly.

Examples:

You might specify that you would not want "artificial feeding".
You might explain what you mean by "terminal".

✔ CHECK IT OUT! ✔

In some states, a "Living Will" is effective only if you've been diagnosed with a terminal illness. Be sure and check with a medical authority or attorney about the laws in your state. Also, your "Living Will" may not be effective if you suffer a stroke, or are in a coma and your condition isn't considered terminal.

For More Help

- Choice in Dying (212-366-5540) will send you sample health care documents and advise you how to correctly fill them out.

- National Hospice Organization (703-243-5900) will help you find Hospice care in your area.

   Check your bookstores for guides to filling out a "Living Will" and appointing a health care proxy. Or call your attorney for assistance.

Disability Planning Is Important

HISTORICAL LANDMARK

How To Make Your "Living Will" Work

1. **Involve The Whole Family**

   All too often, we fill out a "Living Will" without consulting every family member. Your objective should be to discuss the topic well enough that each family member can apply your wishes to whatever situation is at hand.

2. **Find a Doctor Who Will Be Your Advocate**

   A "Living Will" means nothing if a physician won't act on it. Make sure your doctor understands and agrees with the end of life wishes - and would be willing to fight to make sure they are heeded. If the doctor won't agree, find one who will.

3. **Appoint a Health Care Proxy**

   A "Durable Power of Attorney for Health Care" is a document by which you can name a family member or trusted friend (usually called a health care proxy) to make medical decisions for you if you become incapacitated. It also details what the person can and cannot do under what circumstances. In making decisions about end of life issues, most doctors prefer talking face to face with a proxy, instead of having to interpret a "Living Will."

4. **Distribute Both Documents**

   Hospitals or nursing homes cannot honor a "Living Will" or "Power of Attorney" if they don't have a copy of it. Make sure family members, doctors and all medical facilities have copies.

5. **Consider Hospice Care**

   Terminally ill patients who fear the intrusion of high-tech machines may prefer Hospice Care to hospitalization. Although Hospice workers can administer medication, their primary task is to ease, not forestall death, and provide emotional support to patient and family.

From the "Gospel of Caregiving"

Advanced Planning Tools

REPRESENT

A Multitude of Tour Options on Your "Family Care" Journey

Flashback To Childhood:

Remember as a child, how on long trips you would play games to help pass the time. As we move toward more "Advanced Planning Tools", here's a trivia question for you:

"Trivia Question" NAME THAT TUNE!

Name the #1 Hit Music Record in 1949?

ANSWER: You guessed it...
"How Much Is That Doggie in the Window?"

Why this "Trivia Question"?

NO,` your "Family Care" journey hasn't gone to the dogs. The "Trivia Question" appears for a reason. *"Were you able to guess the correct answer?"* If so, you represent a very small fraction of the population.

The same holds true with naming the multitude of planning tools you can use regarding "Advanced Planning". Most people don't have a clue.* However, your estate and financial planners do have the answers. That's why they're important to know.

*For example: To create both an awareness of their existence and to test your knowledge, define the following:

Advanced Planning Tools We Will Explore

→

Pour Over Provisions *(my favorite)* **Joint Ownership** **Community Property** **Beneficlary Designations**

Advanced Planning Tools

"Introducing 4 Advanced Planning Tools"

#1. <u>Pour Over Provisions</u>

a. "Living Trusts" have other estate planning advantages as well. You can use a "Living Trust" to unify your estate's assets under one manager and provide continuing management for your family and other heirs after you're gone.

b. How? In your Will, you can direct that any assets not held in your "Living Trust" be "poured over" to the trust at your death to be managed along with other trust assets.

c. Be aware though, that the assets placed in the trust at your death will be subject to probate.

#2. <u>Joint Ownership</u>

a. Property you and your spouse own jointly with rights of survivorship will pass privately to your spouse outside of probate at your death.

b. Using joint ownership for the family home and a modest bank account or investment portfolio is a simple way to help your family's lives go on as normally as possible while the estate is being settled.

c. Be aware though, that using joint ownership precludes the use of other estate planning techniques that may help to save estate taxes and may have other ramifications for your estate plan.

"Just Ahead"

TOUR BUS

Community Property

Beneficiary Designations

Advanced Planning Tools

More Advanced Planning

#3. Community Property

a. Community property doesn't pass automatically to your spouse.

b. If your state has a community property law, you and your spouse each own a one-half interest in assets acquired during your marriage. (When one spouse dies, the survivor continues owning half of the assets.)

c. The deceased spouse needs a Will to transfer the other half.

Note: If during the marriage, you have acquired assets that you own separately (i.e. gifts and inheritances), you need a Will to determine what will happen to this non-community property.

#4. Beneficiary Designations

a. You may have significant assets that can pass outside of probate by beneficiary designation rather than by Will.

b. Life insurance proceeds, qualified retirement plan benefits, annuities and IRA accounts can go directly to beneficiaries instead of through probate.

115

Estate Planning Strategies

MOUNTAINS AHEAD
Steep Incline
30% Grade

As the "Family Care Roadmap" climbs into Estate Planning Strategies, your speed is reduced. You may even think, "This is like pushing our car up the mountain". (Oh! It's not that bad!) It is slower reading........ but extremely important...... like most of the sights on your journey.

Advanced Planning

The "Advanced Planning" information provided to this point gives you a basic understanding of "estate planning preliminaries". The following tools provide you with various options, regarding how you can plan for assets to pass to those individuals you want and at the least federal estate tax cost.

Credit Shelter By-Pass Trusts

The Two Trust Estate Plan

QTIP Trusts (Should prove interesting)

Life Insurance

Lifetime Gifts to Friends and Family

Approaching The Summit...

"OK... It's a logical question?"

"What is a Credit Shelter or By-Pass Trust?"

a. It's a strategy that can help both you and your spouse take advantage of the unified credit and transfer up to $2 million in assets (in 2006 and later) to your children or other heirs free of federal estate tax.

b. Example: One way to make the most of both your's and your spouse's unified credits is to arrange for your estate to be divided into two parts at your death. One part would pass outright to your spouse.

c. The second part of your estate is placed in a trust created by your Will.

d. This trust can pay your surviving spouse a lifetime income - and then benefit your children or other named beneficiaries after your spouse's death.

e. This strategy can even give your spouse a limited power to withdraw trust assets.

f. At your death, your unified credit will be applied against the assets in the credit shelter trust.

g. If these assets are less than or equal to the unified credit exclusion amount, no estate tax will be due.

h. No tax is due on the assets passing to your spouse, either, because of the unlimited marital deduction.

i. At your spouse's death the credit shelter trust assets will pass to your children or other trust beneficiaries.

j. The assets won't be taxed as part of your spouse's estate.

k. The assets that passed to your spouse under the unlimited marital deduction will be included in your spouse's estate.

l. However, your spouse's unified credit will be available to offset tax on some or all of those assets.

Approching...

**"The Twin Peaks of the
Two Trust Estate Plan"**

What is it?

a. It's another planning strategy for couples that use a credit shelter trust and one other trust.

b. This plan saves estate tax in the same way a credit shelter trust alone does.

c. But, with a "Two Trust Estate Plan", the assets that pass to your spouse under the "marital deduction" are also placed in a trust, rather than left to your spouse. This "marital trust" may be a QTIP trust (explained in the next section), or it can be another trust qualifying for the marital deduction.

d. In general, for property in the marital trust to qualify for the marital deduction:

   • All of the income must be payable to your spouse at least as frequently as annually.

   • If you don't use a QTIP trust as your marital trust, you must also give your surviving spouse a general power to distribute the trust property.

   • You may give your spouse a lifetime power to distribute trust property, or you can give your spouse the power to distribute property only by a Will.

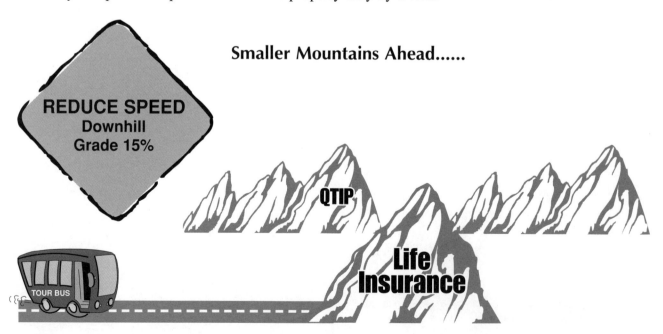

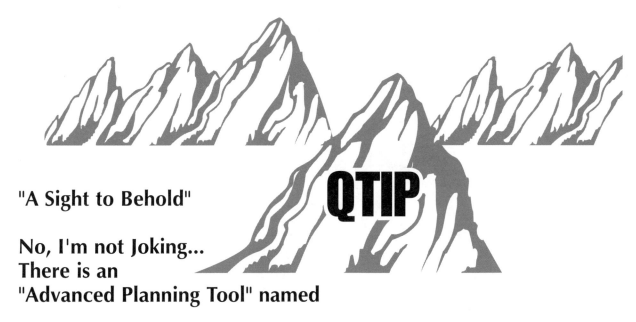

"A Sight to Behold"

No, I'm not Joking...
There is an
"Advanced Planning Tool" named

"QTIP Trust"

Summary

With a "Qualified Terminable Interest Property (QTIP) Trust", you can give your surviving spouse a life income and choose who will receive the property in the trust after your spouse's death - your children or grandchildren, for example.

Your personal representative can elect to claim the marital deduction for the trust property.

For the trust property to be eligible for QTIP election:

- You must give your surviving spouse a qualifying income interest for life.
- Your spouse may not transfer that income interest to anyone else during life or at death.
- The assets may not be distributed to anyone other than your spouse while your spouse is alive.

QTIP Trust assets will be included in your spouse's estate - and your spouse's estate may have to pay estate tax on the assets.

The assets themselves must be distributed as you have directed in your QTIP Trust Agreement.

You retain ultimate control over who receives them.

Life Insurance's Role in Estate Planning

For larger estates that may be subject to tax even when family trusts are used, life insurance can provide the funds needed to pay estate taxes without liquidating estate assets.

If you have a substantial amount of life insurance, you may want to create an Irrevocable Life Insurance Trust to help beneficiaries manage the proceeds and potentially reduce estate taxes.

With a life insurance trust, the trust is the owner and beneficiary of your life insurance policies.

At your death, your trustee collects the proceeds and manages them for the benefit of your family or other beneficiaries.

As long as the trust is properly structured, the insurance proceeds won't be included in your estate for federal estate tax purposes, with one exception: Exception: The proceeds of any insurance policy you transfer to a trust within three years of your death will be included.

You can avoid this three year rule by:

1. Transferring your insurance policies to a trust now, while you're in good health or;

2. Having your trust buy new insurance policies on your life rather than transferring existing policies.

Just ahead.......

"What a Gorgeous View"

Lifetime Gifts to Family and Friends

You don't have to wait until your death to make tax-saving transfers. In fact, a well-planned program of lifetime gifts to family, friends and charity can save estate and gift taxes, preserve more of your assets for your family and other heirs and ensure your property goes to the people you want to have it.

Life Time GIFTS to Family and Friends

1. ## The Gift-Tax Annual Exclusion

   Each year you can give any number of people up to $10,000 each in assets ($20,000 if your spouse joins in the gift) without triggering any federal transfer tax. This annual tax exclusion is available in addition to your unified credit and is adjusted annually for inflation.

2. ## Exclusion for Medical and Tuition Payment

   The tax law also allows you an unlimited exclusion for certain tuition and medical payments made on behalf of others. To qualify for this exclusion, you must make the tuition or medical payments directly to the educational institution or medical facility. Payments for medical insurance qualify for the exclusion. Payments for dormitory fees, books, supplies and similar school expenses do not qualify for the exclusion.

3. ## Gifts to Minors Trust

   Many people don't feel comfortable giving large sums to children or grandchildren. A Living Trust that will hold and manage those sums until the child is maturer may seem like a good idea. However, gifts of "future interests" don't qualify for the annual exclusion. Thus, gift tax is imposed regardless of the amount of the gift.

A better strategy is to create a "Gift to Minors Trust". Gifts to these trusts qualify for the annual exclusions. With a "Gifts to Minors Trust", you can direct your trustee to use the trust income and assets for the child's benefit (i.e. finance his/her college education - until the child reaches age 21). Then, the child must be given the right to all the trust income and assets. However, you can incorporate "Crummey" powers in the "Gifts to Minors Trust" that will give the child only a limited time to withdraw from the trust when he or she reaches age 21.

The Gift That Keeps on Giving

Lifetime Gifts to Family and Friends

4. Crummey Powers

These powers convert a future interest in trust property into a present interest eligible for the annual exclusion. "Crummey Powers" are commonly used to make annual exclusion gifts in trust to children without giving them present rights to the trust property. Example: You could create a trust that gives your adult children no present interests in the trust property other than the right to withdraw each year's amount equal to the gift tax annual exclusion. Your children would not have to exercise the right. Just their having the right to withdraw would be sufficient to allow the annual exclusion for your transfers to the trust. You must notify the trust beneficiaries of the existence of the power. However, you can limit the period during which the power can be exercised.

5. Personal Residence Trusts

Your home maybe the most valuable asset you own. Removing its value from your taxable estate could significantly reduce estate taxes. One method of eventually passing your home on to your children (or other beneficiaries) in a tax favored manner is through the use of a Personal Residence Trust. With a Personal Residence Trust, you irrevocably transfer a personal residence to a Living Trust. You, or you and your spouse retain for a fixed period, the right to use and occupy the residence. At the end of the period, the residence passes to your children (or another beneficiary). The residence placed in the trust need not be your principal residence - a second residence qualifies.

As long as you survive the trust term, the value of the retained right to use the residence plus all appreciation in the home's value after the trust was set up, escape being included in your estate for federal and state purposes.

However, if you die before the end of the trust term, the value of the residence at death is included in the estate for estate tax purposes. In this instance, the trust won't save estate taxes. When the trust ends, you can remain in the home, as long as you pay fair market rent to the new owner.

Be aware that with the trust, from a legal perspective, you are giving away your home. A qualifying trust can provide some flexibility, but your overall control over the residence is limited. Professional tax assistance is essential.

Estate Planning Means   Advanced Planning

Thanks!

You will soon be leaving the rugged majesty of "Estate Planning".

Please feel free to browse through "Charitable Gifts" and "Glossary of Estate Planning Terms".

Charitable Gifts

A. Charitable Remainder Trusts

1. With a Charitable Remainder Trust, you can transfer property to a trust set up for the charity of your choice. The trust pays you, or you and your spouse, or someone else you've chosen, an income for life or a period of years. The trust ends at the death of the last income beneficiary and the charity receives the property.

B. Charitable Lead Trusts

1. If you're currently making regular gifts to a favorite charity - or would like to make regular gifts to a charity - you may find it to your advantage to use a Charitable Lead Trust for those gifts.

2. A Charitable Lead Trust pays income to the charity of your choice for a set period. At the end of that period the trust assets pass to the person you've named as the trust's remainder beneficiary (i.e. your child or grandchild). Both the charity and heirs benefit.

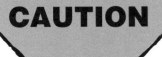

Next.......
Sunglasses....and Sunblock are required as your
next Family Care Journey takes you into some
"Stunning Splendor".

Glossary of Estate Planning Terms

Administrator
   Person appointed by a court to manage the estate of a person who dies without a Will.

Beneficiary
   A person designated to receive the income, principal or proceeds of a trust, estate, insurance policy or retirement plan.

Charitable Trust
   A trust having a charitable organization as a beneficiary.

Corporate Fiduciary
   An institution which acts for the benefit of another. One example is a bank acting as a trustee.

Decedent
   The deceased.

Durable Power of Attorney
   A legal document empowering someone to handle your affairs if you are comatose, mentally incompetent or otherwise incapacitated - but still alive.

Estate
   Your net worth, or everything you own, minus everything you owe.

Estate Administration
   The process of finding out where all the assets and bills are, reading the Will and carrying out wishes of the deceased.

Estate Tax
   The tax paid by the administrator or executor of a person's estate out of the estate's assets.

Executor (or Personal Representative)
   Someone appointed by a person in a Will to carry out the Will's provisions. A "co-executor" acts as executor with another or others.

Fiduciary
   A person in a position of trust or confidence. The fiduciary is bound by duty to act in good faith. Example: trustees, executors and administrators.

Gift Tax
   Tax on gifts generally paid by the person making the gift rather than the recipient.

Gift Tax Annual Exclusion

The provision in the tax law that exempts the first $10,000 (as adjusted for inflation) in present-interest gifts a person gives to each recipient during a year from federal gift taxes.

Gross Estate

The total value of an individual's property for estate tax purposes.

Guardian

A person legally appointed to manage the rights and/or property of a person incapable of taking care of his or her own affairs. A "guardian ad litem" is appointed by the court to prosecute or defend an action for a minor. Also known as "conservator".

Heir

A person entitled to inherit a portion of the estate of a person who has died without a Will.

Interest

Any right in property.

Intestate

Dying without a Will.

Joint Ownership

The ownership of property by two or more persons, usually with the right of survivorship.

Letters Testamentary

Given by the court to the executor, these authorize him or her to manage the affairs of the deceased. These are what the executor takes to the real estate agent, bank and safe deposit box.

Life Insurance Trust

A trust that has the proceeds of a person's life insurance policy as its principal.

Living Trust

A trust that goes into effect while the trust creator is still living.

Living Will

A legal document specifying whether you want your life prolonged by artificial or extraordinary means once you are incapable of making that decision. It can also include your willingness to become an organ donor.

Power of Appointment

The authority given by one person to another under a trust agreement or Will to decide who will receive and enjoy an interest in property.

Power of Attorney

A document which authorizes a person to act as another person's agent.

Probate

A court with the power to probate Wills and settle estates.

Probate Estate

Those estate assets which fall within the jurisdiction of the probate court before being transferred to another person. Life insurance proceeds, for example, are not generally part of the probate estate.

Successor Trustee or Executor

An individual or institution which takes the place of a trustee or executor who can no longer hold office.

Testator

A person who makes or has made a Will.

Testamentary Trust

A trust established in a Will which begins after the testator's death.

Trust

A legal relationship where property is transferred to and managed by another person or institution for the benefit of another person.

Trust Agreement

A document which creates a trust and establishes the rules which control the trust's management.

Unified Credit

A federal tax credit which offsets gift tax and estate tax liability. The unified credit is being increased gradually from $192,800 in 1997 to $345,800 in 2006, which is equivalent to a combined gift and estate tax exclusion of $600,000 in 1997 and $1 million in 2006.

Will

A legally executed document which explains how and to whom a person would like his or her property distributed after death.

Leaving Estate Planning

TOUR BUS

Entering Long Term Care

Part VI

The Stunning Splendor of Long Term Care Insurance

"We're Off to See the Wonderful Wizard..."

LTC

As we continue our "Family Care" journey, we turn off on a yellow brick road that leads us into the land of LTC.........(OR, in our case)

"The Stunning Splendor of Long Term Care Insurance"

Introducing Your Tour Guide

"I am the great and wonderful Wizard"...... "To enter "The Stunning Splendor of Long Term Care Insurance" please answer the following questions:"

1. QUESTION: Home health care and Hospice care are increasingly becoming alternatives to nursing home care. More than 60% of all long term care is now provided outside a nursing home? True or False?

    ANSWER: False - 80% of all long term care is provided outside a nursing home.

2. QUESTION: More than 10 million families currently provide informal, unpaid care for an older parent or relative, a number that has tripled in the past 10 years? True or False?

    ANSWER: False - 22 million families provide informal, unpaid care to older parents and relatives.

3. QUESTION: Long Term Care benefits are payable when you're unable to perform two or more Activities of Daily Living (ADL's) or have a severe Cognitive Impairment - and you aren't required to submit receipts for services? True or False?

    ANSWER: True

4. QUESTION: Long Term Care policies recognize six ADL's: bathing, dressing, transferring, toileting, continence, and eating. Bathing and dressing are the most common LTC limitations, experienced by 80 to 90% of those receiving care? True or False?

    ANSWER: True

Long Term Care Insurance

"The wonderful Wizard" says, "continue answering the following questions before entering......"

"The Stunning Splendor of Long Term Care Insurance"

6. QUESTION: You do not receive your total monthly benefit amount if it exceeds your incurred expenses? True or False?

    ANSWER: False - You do receive your total monthly benefit, even if it exceeds your incurred expenses.

7. QUESTION: There is no coordination of benefits with Medicare or other insurance. This means you receive a monthly LTC check in addition to any other long term care income you're receiving? True or False?

    ANSWER: True

8. QUESTION: If you recover before using all your benefits, you will have access to the money that remains if you experience a recurrence? True or False?

    ANSWER: True

"You Ask The Wise Wizard"...

Long Term Care Insurance is Disability Based. You qualify for benefits when you require substantial assistance with two out of six activities of daily living (ADL's), or suffer severe cognitive impairment that requires substantial supervision. Long Term Care Insurance pays for key services such as:

- **Home Health Care**   • **Assisted Living**   • **Nursing Home**

"The Magnificent Wizard".........

Defines

"Activities of Daily Living" (ADL's)

- Bathing
- Dressing
- Transferring
- Toileting
- Continence
- Eating

OR......

"Cognitive Impairment"
"A deterioration or loss in your intellectual capacity which requires another person's assistance."

Long Term Care Insurance

"The Caring Wizard Says".........

"You Are Now Entering The City Of........."

Long Term Care Insurance

Population:
"Fastest growing...quickly becoming an insurance policy that every individual and family must have."

"The Wizard asks.....Did You Know?"

- Activities of Daily Living (ADL's) are the most widely accepted measure of an individual's ability to live independently.

- With cognitive impairment, a loss in your intellectual capacity can result from Alzheimer's disease or similar forms of senility, irreversible dementia or advanced age.

"Most Likely, You'll Need Long Term Care Insurance!"

Reason 1: <u>It's Importance is Increasing</u>
- If you want to preserve financial security and independence in the event of an extended disability.
- It's not just for the elderly, because many working age adults have disabling injuries and illnesses as well.

<u>**FACT:**</u>
Persons between the ages of 18 to 64 represent 40% of those who currently need LTC. Currently, there are 12 million people of all ages who need help with activities of daily living.

Reason 2: <u>More Than Likely You'll Need Long Term Care</u>
- What are the real risks? There is a 1 in 88 risk of needing home owners insurance; a 1 in 47 chance of having an auto accident and a 2 in 5 chance of needing long term care.
- About 60% of the U.S. population will need long term care at some point.

"These Reasons Are Important"

Reason 3: <u>Today's Long Term Care Insurance Offers More Care Choices:</u>
- It offers a full spectrum of care options:
  - home care*   - assisted living facility   - nursing home
  - adult day care   - foster care

* The policy may offer professional home care, which must be provided by a licensed home health care agency or total home care, in which family, friends or licensed home health care agencies can provide care.

Reason 4: <u>If You Become Disabled for any Reason and Couldn't Live Independently, How Would You Pay For the Care You Need?</u>
- The financial impact of Long Term Care is significant, no matter where it is provided, and government programs don't always pay for services.
  - Nursing home care now costs $30,000 - $40,000 per year, while home care can cost $1,000 plus each month or $12,000 plus per year. Assisted living costs about $2,000 per month, or $24,000 per year.
  - Medicare pays only 16% of all long term care in the U.S. today. When it does, it covers only skilled or acute nursing care. State Medicaid programs cover 38%. You are required, however, to spend down to poverty levels to qualify for assistance.
  - A large number of individuals who need Long Term Care, about 33%, must rely on their own savings or family help to meet expenses.

Reason 5: <u>It Protects You:</u>
- Long Term Care Insurance protects against the high cost of an extended illness or injury by paying benefits, if you are unable to function independently.
- Most plans cover care either at home or in a facility.
- Vouchers for the reimbursement of expenses are not required, as a fixed rate is paid monthly, once service begins.
- You don't have to be hospitalized in order to receive benefits.

Reason 6: <u>It Helps You Both Financially and Emotionally:</u>
- Pays monthly benefits.
- Provides 24 hour referral service about financial and long term care services.
- Offers Respite Care Benefits......which allow care providers time off.

The LTC Hotline......
"Looking for a Long-Term Care Policy?"

The Wise Wizard says:

Make Sure the Policy

1. Covers skilled nursing care, custodial care, all nursing-home services and home based care.

2. Will pay benefits on at least $110 per day.

3. Contains an automatic cost of living increase clause pegged to inflation.

4. Has the shortest possible waiting period before benefits begin.

5. Provides at least three years' coverage with a longer period preferred.

6. Covers a comprehensive list of "triggering events". Triggering events are conditions, such as Alzheimer's disease, that cause the start of benefit payments.

7. Offers a waiver of premiums should you be confined to a nursing home.

8. Won't be cancelled as you age or if you become ill or injured.

9. Won't increase your premiums as you age.

The Stunning Splendor of Long Term Care Insurance

The Long Term Care Assessment

What is it?

It's a conversation between a trained assessor and you (or your older loved one) which includes questions covering:

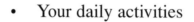

- Your daily activities

- Household chores

- Transportation

- Meal preparation

- Your past and present health

- Medication(s) you're currently taking

- Recent visits to your physician

- A blood pressure reading

- Measuring your height and weight

Uh, oh...maybe I did something wrong with that last spell!

There will also be questions designed to test your cognitive abilities. You'll probably find that many of the questions are basic and have obvious answers. The Long Term Care Assessment generally takes less than 30 minutes.

It doesn't take long in "The Stunning Splendor of Long Term Care Insurance..."

"Your Pot of Gold
At The End of the Rainbow"

Long Term Care Insurance

Without question, Long Term Care (LTC) Insurance is becoming increasingly important not only to older loved ones, but to all baby-boomer aged families.

Tax advantages provided by recent health care legislation make the purchase of qualified LTC insurance attractive for both employers and employees. Provisions differ depending on the tax payer.

- ### All Companies

  Employers have the option of covering only certain employee classes. The employee and employee's spouse can be covered, and both receive the same tax advantages. Because employer paid premiums are not included in an employee's gross income, they are not inputted as income to the employee.

- ### C - Corporations

  A corporate employer generally can take a business expense deduction for the amount of LTC premiums paid for both employees and their spouses.

- ### Self Employed Individuals

  Self employed individuals and their spouses can deduct a percentage of their eligible LTC premiums. The percentage will increase over time, for example:

Year	Eligible Deduction
1997	40%
2003	80%
2007	100%

- ### Individual Purchases

  Medical and dental expenses can now include eligible LTC premiums as part of their medical expenses.

Leaving Long Term Care

TOUR BUS

Entering Housing Options

NOTES

Part VII

The Majestic Grandeur
Of Housing Options

"The Majestic Grandeur of Housing Options"

The last stop of your "Family Care" journey takes you into the multi-faceted and complex world of "Housing Options".

Before entering the "majestic grandeur" of this vast area, we need to understand one critically important point......which is:

The Significance of the Home

Home, for most people, is a very sacred place. Our roots and identity are tied to it. This is especially true when it comes to our parents and older loved ones. Thus, when it comes to considering a change of residence and / or moving, this act in itself generates tremendous emotional and grief responses.

Why Does This Happen?

Because staying at home and remaining independent are among our older loved ones fiercest desires. This is essential to understand. Most have lived in their homes a long time and do not want to move. This is "their house". In reality, it is sacred to them. It is a place called home.

To Understand this Point Even More......

We Need to Closely Look at our Parents and Older Loved Ones.....

Who are OFTEN Called........

"A People of Resilience"

Next... | Housing Side Tour

Housing Option SIDE TRIP "Memory Lane"

"A People of Resilience"

Profile

They may appear older today......even frail. Yet, our parents, siblings and older relatives are a *"people of resilience"*. Their faces may showcase wrinkles. Their skin may feature a "weathered look". They may seem tired and worn.

Don't Be Fooled! Underneath these surface features, you'll find character, wisdom and a "gigantic heart". Try visualizing them in such terms as:

Vitality......Strength.......Productive.......Ambitious........

We share the same values. Yet, far too often, we see these generations in a far different light. In reality we should call them "The Pioneers of Change", for what they've experienced has been simply amazing.

Tired of Horse and Buggy?
Try the Model T.

Better yet, take a quick trip into outerspace.
Or, even cyberspace.

In the dark?
Light a candle, or flip a switch into a world of
Lights, television and computers.

Pony Express too slow?
Pick up the phone and call long distance.

Want to know about War and Peace?
Boom.......Bust?

> # Today's Seniors have SEEN IT ALL.
>
> # They Are Truly A People Of Resilience.

A People of Resilience

They're called this, because of how they've handled and adjusted to change. Should they move from their homes, this resilience will continue. Our older loved ones are strong and proud. Given time, most do adjust to moving.... But, keep in mind, this creates grief. If possible, give your older loved one (even parents) time to adjust before a move.

Were You Aware.... That The "People of Resilience" Have A Story to Tell?

They certainly do. In fact, our older loved ones have many tales to tell.   It's called.....

Oh, no! Here comes that same old story again.

<u>REMINISCING</u>

We may think, "here comes that same old story again. But, it's not so!" The opportunity to reminisce can help our elders unlock what may be long forgotten resources within them. Reminiscing plays a key role in our older loved one's adjustment to emotional and grief responses.

<u>It's Important to Reminisce</u>

In our later years of life, reminiscing helps us come to terms with events and feelings that we may not have had time to reflect upon or think through when they occurred. It helps us remember a time when:

- We felt strong and capable

- When we overcame problems

- When we made difficult choices

- When we dealt with losses

"Reminiscing Can Fill Us With A SENSE of Power and Capability".......

140

 "Pioneers of Change"

Importance of Reminiscing to the Older Person

- Helps to maintain self-esteem and reinforces a sense of identity.

- Provides a sense of achievement and pleasure.

- Gains status by revealing selected elements of his/her life history.

- Strengthens coping skills related to the aging process.

- Places past experiences in perspective.

- Releases emotions such as grief.

- Establishes a common ground for communication.

- Promotes mental and emotional well-being.

- Combats isolation, loneliness and depression.

> ### "Reminiscing"
>
> A way of reliving, re-experiencing or savoring events of the past that are personally significant.

Why is Reminiscing Important to You?

- Helps with knowledge and understanding about the older person and their time period.

- Builds a bridge between past experiences and the present.

- Establishes a mutually satisfying relationship through sharing of information and experiences.

- Provides an insight for gaining cues about the person's behavior in the present.

Reminiscing

Research has shown that older people who go through life review are less withdrawn and apathetic. Reminiscing helps older persons get back in touch with things that matter to them (like home) and once again experience positive feelings about themselves.

From the "Gospel of Caregiving"

Housing Side Trip

Next..."The Art of Listening..."

Reminiscing.........

"The Art of Listening Involves You"

Steps for Reminiscing

1. Think of some open ended questions you might ask to start the conversation.

2. Listen actively. Maintain eye contact. Use your body to communicate your acceptance and attention. Lean slightly toward your older loved one. Nod your head. Don't interrupt.

3. Respond positively. Give feedback by making caring, appropriate comments that encourage the person to continue.

4. Ask follow-up questions. Restate key points to indicate your understanding, to clarify what has been said, or to guide the conversation.

Reminiscing Can Be A Wonderful Experience.......

- Take Time to Listen
- Show an Interest
- Ask Questions
- Express Feelings
- Give Your Loved One Time to Reflect
- Encourage Them to Write or Tape a Family History

Reminiscing

Reminiscing plays a key role in the decision process. It's a way of reaching back and moving forward.

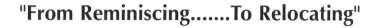

"From Reminiscing.......To Relocating"

Moving To A New Residence?

Even if your parents or older loved ones have been part of the decision making process and have been looking forward to a move, keep in mind the "Significance of Home". Moving does create grief. It does require an adjustment time.

Highly Recommended

When considering a move, please:

- Encourage open communication
- Express feelings
- Include them in activities
- Give them responsibilities
- Join together in mutual problem solving
- Support them in making new friends
- Allow them time to reminisce

Your "Housing Options" tour is just ahead. It will take you into the following areas:

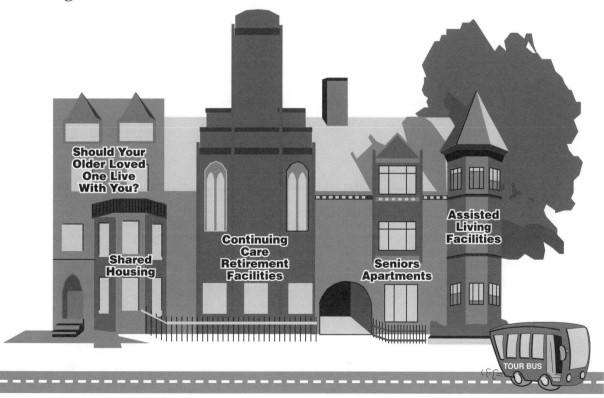

Should Your Older Loved One Live With You?

Shared Housing

Continuing Care Retirement Facilities

Seniors Apartments

Assisted Living Facilities

TOUR BUS

143

"Entering The Majestic Grandeur of Housing Options"

Announcement

Your "Family Care' journey continues. This guided tour explores "Housing Options". It is especially designed for "The People of Resilience" and their adult children.

Housing

Housing is always a question at some point for most older adults and their family members. There are no hard and fast rules about individuals moving into optional housing. However, eventually most individuals and/or couples must at least look at what's available.

Family Care Observations

As this guided tour of housing options begins, keep in mind that housing help is least available when it's most urgently needed.   It is highly recommended that housing options be explored early.

Suggested Guidelines:

• Don't wait until a health crisis to begin planning.

• Remember, some housing options require that the resident must be in good health.

• Investigate all facilities, if possible. Invite family members. The best way to tell the well-run homes, apartments and facilities from the badly run ones, is to be your own consumer watchdog and spend some time there.

........Next.......

Housing
Bonus Tour

It's A Delicate Family Issue

To Move Or Not To Move...?
That Is The Question

Question

Helping your older loved ones (even parents) make decisions about housing is a delicate issue. There are numerous questions involved, including "how do you know if your parents would be happier in a new or smaller place, even with assistance?"

TOUR RECOMMENDATIONS

? ? ?

To answer the "above question", plan to spend more time with your parents or older loved ones. On these occasions, make it a point to observe what may be OK or not be OK.

- If you wonder about your parent's ability to prepare meals, visit right before dinner.

- Are they having trouble getting around?

- Look for their mobility and their ability to handle daily chores and activities.

- Take time to talk to family members or friends who see your older loved one(s) more frequently or even less frequently. They may be better able to convey to you the "real" status of your loved one.

- Look for clues. Parents and loved ones will often drop hints that they do need help and that they're receptive to moving.

Just Ahead
Historical Marker

145

Helping Your Loved Ones Decide Housing Options

Hear ye..... Hear ye...... Rules of Engagement......

- Keep in mind that your parents and older loved ones have probably given this a lot more thought than you realize, regardless of whether they want to talk about it.

- Remember the grief that's involved. Both you and your older loved ones will be dealing with loss. This includes your loss of the parents who took care of you and their loss of their own independence and former lives. There's a great deal of pain involved.

- Be aware that your parent's basic personality patterns and traits don't change. In fact, they may even intensify as they age. A parent who generally did not talk about feelings or needing help, probably will not do so now. Don't see this as your failure to communicate.

- Regardless of what you may think and feel, you're not in charge. Even if everything seems up to you, your parents are still in control. They need to be involved in the decision making process.

- Ease into conversations informally. Try not to preach or overreact. Talk about a friend or relative who is undergoing the same decisions. Ask "how do you want to handle this, if and when you decide it's time to move?"

- Another communication tool is to mention your specific concern. "I'm worried about your ability to maintain the house, etc.".

- Offer information and solutions instead of conclusions. Convey your willingness to actively take a role in the process. Or, bring in a trusted outsider (friend, doctor, clergy, etc.) to offer support in the conversation.

- Give your parents and older loved ones time to think and react to new ideas. That's why early communication and planning before a need or crisis arise are so critically important.

- Most important - listen to and for their real concerns. You may be trying to reassure them on one thing, when they're really worried about something else, like never seeing their circle of friends anymore.

From the "Gospel of Caregiving"

Next...
Tour
Stop #1

Housing Options......

Should Your Older Loved One Live With You?

One housing option that needs to be examined early between older family members (including parents) and adult children is the question of "Should They Come Live With You?" This is not an easy question to answer, since there are both advantages and disadvantages. The following summary will help walk you through the numerous questions that require answers. Your joint decision will, to a large extent, be determined by how you respond to the questions.

Advantages:

- Combined expenses.

- Companionship for your loved one.

- Household tasks are combined under one roof.

- Peace of mind knowing your loved one is safe and secure.

Disadvantages:

- Tension having a loved one live with you.

- Compromised privacy.

- Your loved one's lifestyle and needs may conflict with your own.

- Your loved one may feel restricted in the new surroundings.

Should Your Older Loved One Live With You?

✔ Your Checklist ✔

- How do you feel your own life is going? Are you under stress from work, marriage, financial difficulties or family problems? How is your health? Your spouse's?

- What effect will this have on your relationship with others? For example, how do your spouse and your children feel about the possibility?

- Can your home accommodate another adult? Will your loved one have a separate bedroom?

- Is your home safe and accessible for your older family member? Does he/she have a handicap, which will necessitate physical changes in your house? Are there stairs your loved one has to climb? Can he or she easily go outdoors if this is desirable?

- What type of assistance will you have to provide now and in the future? Talk to your loved one's physician.

- If you are going to need assistance caring for your older loved one, is it available in your community? How much does it cost? Can you and your older loved one afford to pay for it?

- If you work full time, who will care for your loved one when you are at your job?

- Is your immediate family prepared and willing to assist you? Specifically, what support are they prepared to give you?

- If you take responsibility for becoming the primary family caregiver for your older loved one, can you expect to receive financial or other assistance from family members?

- What impact will this have on your leisure time, vacations, time with friends and social activities? How will you manage to preserve opportunities for these valuable experiences?

- Do you have a good relationship with your loved one? Does your spouse? Do your children?

- Do you have a backup plan in the event that you are unable to provide regular care for your loved one?

**Your Answers
Will Guide You in the Decision
Making Process.**

Now Arriving at......Housing Options

Tour Stop #2

SHARED HOUSING
(Also called Group-shared, Supportive and Matched Housing)

Tour Includes:

I. **Overview:** In a shared, group-shared or supportive residence, typically organized by an agency or nonprofit group, up to 20 people share a house and its expenses, chores and management.

Matched housing is a private arrangement in which a parent rents to a college student or healthier elderly person in exchange for help.

II. **Best candidate:** Someone who wants some daily help and companionship, but is still mobile.

III. **Services:** Group-shared residences usually offer meals, housekeeping and transportation; all arranged by a concierge-style live-in manager. Residents pitch in as they can.

Matched arrangement details what renter will do for the elder resident - for instance, laundry, driving, cooking - in exchange for rent.

IV. **Costs:** Group-shared rents (plus utilities) are $4,800 to $6,000 a year, plus about $2,400 per year for food and housekeeping. Low-income elderly should see if they qualify for vouchers known as Section 8 certificates, which help with rent. Contact the local housing authority.

V. **Drawbacks:** For some, the experience of sharing a house is jarring after years of living independently.

For More Help

Call the National Shared Housing Resource Center (431 Pine St., Burlington, VT 05401; 802-862-2727). They can point you toward shared housing in your area or help you organize your own shared situation.

"Coming Up Next.........."

Housing Options

SENIOR APARTMENTS
(Senior apartments: also called seniors-retirement, public and Section 202 housing)

Tour Includes:

I. Overview: Elderly-only complexes that range from garden-style to high-rise. Senior-retirement housing usually offers some services, while the government-run public apartments and government-financed, non-profit-operated Section 202 projects usually don't.

II. Best candidate: A close-to-independent elder who wants privacy but is low income or no longer wants to manage a single-family home.

III. Services: Some seniors-retirement complexes offer meals, transportation, housecleaning, wellness programs and weekly outings, either paid as part of rent or through separate fees. Some Section 202 projects have a coordinator to arrange services.

IV. Costs: In seniors-retirement housing, a modest one-bedroom might rent for $9,600 per year; luxury apartment with services might be $18,000. Public and Section 202 projects charge no more than 30 percent of income; parent's income can be no greater than 30 percent of local median.

V. Drawbacks: Some apartments are dated, cramped and not air-conditioned (though others are spacious, well maintained and elderly-accessible). Public and Section 202 apartments have waits of up to four years.

VI. For more help: Contact your local housing authority or regional Housing and Urban Development office. Local newspaper's health section will sometimes advertise senior apartment projects.

Housing Terms You Should Know

Continuum of Care: A range of care stretching from private apartments with no services to a skilled nursing facility. This system allows residents to move from independent living residences to apartments or rooms with more healthcare support as their needs grow.

From the "Gospel of Caregiving"

"We Are Now Approaching"

Tour Stop #4

CONTINUING-CARE RETIREMENT COMMUNITIES
(Also called life-care communities)

I. **Overview:** Large complexes that offer lifelong care. Residents must be healthy at first, then are moved between their apartment, an assisted-living unit and the "infirmary" (i.e., in-house nursing home) as health needs warrant. Settings range from high rise to campus-like. Dining halls range from sit-down restaurant to cafeteria.

II. **Best candidate:** Middle-to-high-income people who are currently healthy. A few complexes will accept patients with health problems, but then will charge extra when nursing home care is required. ·

III. **Services:** Everything: meals, medical care, housekeeping and social activities. Many also have exercise facilities, library, beauty shop and barber, plus other amenities.

IV. **Costs:** Payment is a combination of entrance fees, monthly rents and medical fees. Typical for a one-bedroom apartment: $80,000 entrance fee and $1,200 a month rent with all medical fees covered; or $40,000 fee, $750 a month rent, but all medical fees extra.

V. **Drawbacks:** Steep entrance fees. (Some families use proceeds from house sale to cover it) Also, some financial risk: If the complex goes bankrupt, residents get money back only after all lenders are paid. For safety's sake, you might have an accountant evaluate the organization's fiscal health before signing up.

VI. **For more help:** The American Association of Homes for the Aging (901 E. St. NW, Suite 500, Washington, D.C. 20004-2037) publishes two good resources: CCRCS - A Guidebook for Consumers ($5) and The Consumer's Directory of CCRS ($24.95), which lists costs and services at 300 complexes. Call 202-508-9442 to order.

Housing Terms You Should Know

Endowment: A payment that secures living space in a retirement community, but does not grant ownership of property. A substantial portion is usually refundable when the resident moves out or dies.

From the "Gospel of Caregiving"

"Growing both in popularity and numbers...... our 5th stop is the Housing Tour's Feature Attraction"

Starring: "ASSISTED LIVING"

I. **Overview:** Assisted Living offers less intense care than nursing homes, but more intense care than shared housing or seniors apartments. Facilities range from ultra modern centers, to resident converted hotels to large homes. Assisted living provides more privacy and independence than nursing homes.

II. **Best candidate:** Someone who needs help with personal care, but doesn't need round-the-clock skilled nursing care. Conditions like incontinence, dementia and being wheelchair-bound can demand more attention than some facilities can give.

III. **Services:** In some facilities, meal preparation and laundry service only; in others, help in dressing, grooming, bathing, taking medications, getting to and from a wheelchair and going to the bathroom. Nursing homes take over when residents need skilled nursing care.

IV. **Costs:** Huge range - from $7,300 a year for room and minimal service to $36,500 a year for near-nursing home level of care. Some states now allow Medicaid to help pay, though funding is limited. Also, some facilities set aside units for low-income seniors. Average monthly rent is approximately $1,800.

V. **Drawbacks:** Lack of on-site medical facilities means elders must move when their health needs grow too large. In most areas, few agencies have a complete listing of available facilities.

VI. **Payment:** Traditionally has been by families. Long Term Care Insurance is now a viable payer source.

For More Help

The Assisted Living Facility Association of America will send you a consumer checklist for how to evaluate facilities. Write to the organization at 9401 Lee Highway, Suite 402, Fairfax, VA 22031.

From the "Gospel of Caregiving"

"Assisted Living"............
Like Long Term Care Insurance.....
It's On The Rise!

Current / Projected Assisted Living Beds in USA	
Year	Projected Number of Beds
1997	199,584
1998	256,720
1999	314,910
2005	665,110

"FLASH!....Breaking Story from Washington"

US Census Report says, "The 85 plus age group will grow from 3.1 million (1990) to 4.3 million by year 2000."

The report also states, "that 50% of the 85 plus group will need help with one or more "Activities of Daily Living" (ADL's).

This stat will impact most families. Stay tuned for more Breaking News....Family Care Reporter.

Housing Terms You Should Know

Long Term Care: 24 hour assistance on a long term basis.

- **Personal Care:**
  General medical assistance, but residents handle daily activities such as meal preparation and house cleaning independently.

- **Intermediate Care:**
  Assistance with activities of daily living with intermittent 24 hour nursing available, and access to emergency care.

- **Skilled Care:**
  24 hour nursing for patients with critical care needs can include physical therapy and other rehabilitation services.

From the "Gospel of Caregiving"

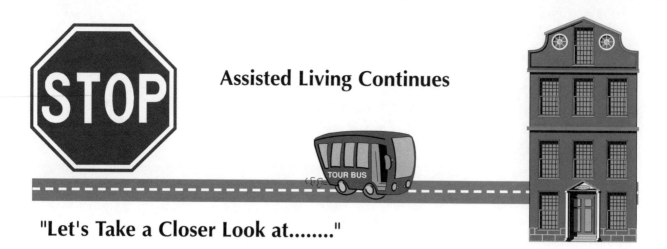

"Let's Take a Closer Look at........"

"Assisted Living Admission Criteria"
(Sample Document Only)

Assisted Living is designed to be a non-medical, independent living arrangement for individuals desiring accommodations which promote opportunities to socialize with others, and which provide limited assistance, when necessary, to maximize independent functioning. Individuals may periodically experience forgetfulness, or mild confusion which does not prevent safe independent care and well-being. Should this become routine to the extent that the resident is incapable of caring for self independently and in a safe manner, or to the extent that intervention by trained personnel becomes necessary, then the resident or legal representative agrees to seek a supervised living agreement.

The following criteria may be used to identify those individuals appropriate for assisted living admission. Appropriate individuals are those who are able to perform the following tasks:

1. Able to take own medications unless applicable regulations permit staff to administer medications (staff may assist in opening bottles, reading instructions or providing reminders).

2. Able to perform with limited assistance own activities of daily living (such as eating, dressing and bathing).

3. Able to select foods from menu in order to maintain a reasonably balanced diet. When on a therapeutic diet, is able to select foods consistent with this prescription.

4. Able to attend meals in a communal setting. In the event of temporary illness, room service is available at an additional charge.

5. May require assistance with eating, such as cutting meat or opening cartons and may use self-help feeding devices.

6. Able to make own arrangements for services necessary to maintain independent functioning.

MORE CRITERIA AHEAD

Assisted Living "To become a resident, you've got to know the criteria....."

Housing Option FEATURE ATTRACTION

7.   May need periodic assistance with transportation outside of the center (Facility may or may not provide such transportation).

8.   The resident must either be continent of bowel and bladder or able to control occasional incontinence of bladder by use of incontinence products. The resident may have an ostomy if they can care for it themselves.

9.   The resident may be unable to walk independently, but is able to move from place to place, including self-transfer and self-evacuate, with assistive devices as approved by the facility.

10. The resident should not routinely require assistance during nighttime sleeping hours.

11. The resident may periodically experience forgetfulness, or mild confusion. Should this forgetfulness or confusion become a routine occurrence to the extent that the resident is incapable of caring for self independently and in a safe manner, or to the extent that intervention by trained personnel becomes necessary, then the resident or legal representative agrees to seek a supervised living arrangement.

12. The resident may not require treatment for drug abuse or dependency, including alcohol.

13. The resident must be free from communicable diseases.

14. The resident must not require the services of licensed personnel provided by the facility.

15. The resident may be blind and/or hearing or speech impaired but able to manage self independently within the environment.

16. The facility does not provide professional nursing or other medical services except as indicated above.

17.   The facility does not provide supervision of the resident. The resident may enter or leave the unit as the resident so desires. The facility requests the resident to sign out/sign in; however, this procedure is voluntary with the resident and the facility will not compel the resident to follow such procedure.

Your Personalized Guided Tour of "Assisted Living"

continues...

"How Much Does It Cost?...."

Sample Illustration of Assisted Living Services & Rate Schedule

- 24-hour personal care assistance

- Emergency call button in each suite and bathroom

- Medication supervision

- 3 Nutritious home-cooked meals served daily

- Bathing and dressing assistance

- Reminders for meals, activities and appointments

- Social programs and activities

- Transportation to scheduled medical appointments, shopping, and social events

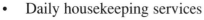

- Daily housekeeping services

- Weekly linen service

- All utilities except private phone and cable

- On-site Beauty/Barber shop

Accommodations and Prices:

Companion Living $1,550.00/month
Standard Accommodations $2,139.00/month
Suite Accommodations $2,356.00/month
Personal Laundry Service . . . .$ 30.00/month

Adult Day Care

Full Day Program . . . .$30.00 (includes 2 meals)
Half Day Program . . . .$20.00 (includes 1 meal)

Congratulations!
You've Been Accepted as an Official Resident......

Certificate of Residency

Sample Illustration
Assisted Living Checklist
For New Residents

Physician's Orders Required:

History & Physical
Complete list of all current medications (including as needed medications)
Order to admit facility
TB test

Personal Items to Bring:

Medications must be in original prescription bottles (no exceptions)
Assistive Devices (shower bench, walker, wheel chair, etc.)
Toiletries (soap, Kleenex, shampoo, etc.)
Hamper or Laundry Bag
Television

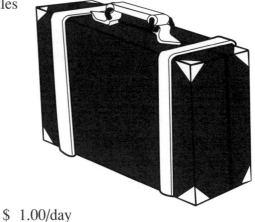

Special Services With Additional Charge:

Personal Laundry Services	$ 1.00/day
Beauty Shop Services:	
Shampoo & Set	$12.00
Color	$ 1.00/weekly
	$15.00/6 months
	$20.00 Peroxide
Cut	$ 8.00
Permanent	$40.00
Guest Meals	$ 4.00/each

Leaving Housing Options

TOUR BUS

Entering Nursing Home (Extended Care)

Your "Family Care Roadmap" Journey Is Almost Complete

Did You Know?

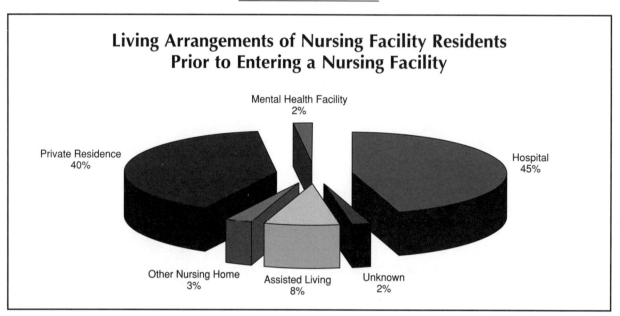

Living Arrangements of Nursing Facility Residents Prior to Entering a Nursing Facility

Mental Health Facility
2%

Private Residence
40%

Hospital
45%

Other Nursing Home
3%

Assisted Living
8%

Unknown
2%

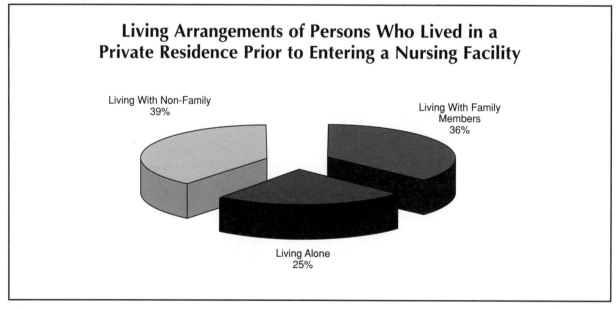

Living Arrangements of Persons Who Lived in a Private Residence Prior to Entering a Nursing Facility

Living With Non-Family
39%

Living With Family Members
36%

Living Alone
25%

Tour Tidbit

Nearly Two Million Persons Aged 65+
Live In Nursing Facilities

Next...Paying for the Services

Financing A Nursing Home Stay

We've learned throughout our "Family Care" tour that there are numerous care and service options available to families. That's the good news.

The difficult question and issue for family members is how to pay for these services. Extended care costs represent such a concern.

A Nursing Home Stay

- Few things can obliterate an estate faster than the need for long term care in a nursing home.

- Steps can be taken to limit the financial drain of caring for an incapacitated loved one.

Steps and Strategy

I. Build an Estate
   a. The more investments and pensions that are available to pay for unexpected long term care, the easier it will be to work out a viable solution.

II. Consider Long Term Insurance
   a. Recap: Medicare is not designed for long-term care. Medicaid can be used only after families have "spent down" much of their savings.
   b. Private Long Term Care Insurance is a key bridge to trust and estate strategies.
   c. Most experts recommend that you choose a policy that begins paying benefits whenever a "cognitive impairment" makes it necessary, or when you can no longer perform two of the following activities: eating, dressing, bathing, moving around and routine necessities of life.
   d. Keep in mind that 70% of patients in nursing homes have Alzheimer's disease, so make sure it's covered.
   e. Make sure that a hospital stay isn't required before long-term care benefits become available. Many illnesses, such as Alzheimer's disease, don't require hospitalization.

"Throughout your "Family Care" journey, the emphasis has been on planning, organizing and communicating. This importance is underscored when considering extended nursing home care for a loved one."

Extended Care

Financing
Nursing Home Care........

III. <u>Find a Good Insurance Broker</u>
   a. A good broker can help you find the best policy for your needs.
   b. Don't use an agent, because he/she represents just one company.
   c. A broker can help you pick a policy from any company that will serve you best.
   d. Make sure the broker knows how to use the services of A.M. Best, Moody's, Standard and Poor's or Comdex to gauge the strength of insurance companies.

IV. <u>Check Whether the Insurance Company is Committed to Providing Long-Term Care Coverage</u>
   a. Has the company been doing it successfully for several years?
   b. Is it licensed to offer coverage in many states?
   c. AARP publishes a helpful guide to long-term care insurance. This guide estimates that a couple age 65 will pay $5,200 per year for coverage. At age 79, they would pay $17,000.
   d. Some companies will insure up to age 84. Most companies stop selling policies at age 80. If you buy before that age you are covered for life.

V. <u>Find a Good Attorney</u>
   a. Establish a relationship with an attorney who is a member of the American Academy of Estate Planning Attorneys and who devotes a good portion of time to estate planning.
   b. The idea is to find strategies that will allow you or an older loved one to turn to Medicaid if necessary, yet still retain as much of the estate as is legally possible for survivors.

VI. <u>Utilize the Services of a Nursing Home Placement Service</u>
   a. These services are designed to bring together resources and information needed by you as you search for a quality nursing home. These services provide detailed reports on the history of every certified nursing home in the country. Call your local area agency on aging or medical social worker for information.

Coming Up Next: ✔ Nursing Home Checklist ✔

TOUR BUS

✔ Nursing Home Checklist ✔

Nursing Home: Involves full-time residence and includes room and board, monitoring, personal assistance, nursing and other health services for persons who are too frail to live independently. Fee basis.		
QUESTIONS TO CONSIDER:	**YES**	**NO**
Is the facility Medicare and/or Medicaid certified?		
Is the home clean and odor free?		
Are residents alert, well groomed, clean and well fed?		
Is there an adequate staff-to-resident ratio?		
Is there a staff dietician? Special dietary meals?		
Is there an activity coordinator?		
Is there a system to protect wanderers?		
Will you need to do personal laundry for your loved one?		
Will you be informed in writing of any billing changes?		
Is there a council for residents?		
Can residents decorate their rooms with their own furniture and personal effects?		

Additional Questions to Consider

- What levels of care are available?

- What are the visitation rules?

- How many residents share a bathroom?

- Are bathrooms equipped with handrails, etc. and other safety features?

Did You Know?

A large number of nursing home residents are Alzheimer's patients. Included on the next several pages is information about "Alzheimer's".

ALZHEIMER'S DISEASE FACT SHEET

Definition and scope:

Alzheimer's Disease (pronounced Altz-hi-merz) is a progressive, degenerative disease that attacks the brain and results in impaired memory, thinking and behavior. It affects an estimated 4 million American adults. It is the most common form of dementing illness. More than 100,000 die of Alzheimer's Disease annually, which makes it the fourth leading cause of death in adults, after heart disease, cancer and stroke.

Symptoms:

Symptoms of Alzheimer's Disease include a gradual memory loss, decline in ability to perform routine tasks, impairment of judgement, disorientation, personality change, difficulty in learning, and loss of language skills. There is variation in the rate of change from person to person. The disease eventually renders its victims totally incapable of caring for themselves.

Cause(s) and Research:

The cause of Alzheimer's Disease is not known and is currently receiving intensive scientific investigation. Suspected causes include a genetic predisposition, slow virus or other infectious agents, environmental toxins and immunologic changes. Other factors also are under investigation.

Scientists are applying the newest knowledge and research techniques in molecular genetics, pathology, virology, immunology, toxicology, neurology, psychiatry, pharmacology, biochemistry and epidemiology to find the cause, treatment, and cure for Alzheimer's Disease and related disorders.

Diagnosis:

There is no single clinical test to identify Alzheimer's Disease. Before diagnosis of the disease is made, other conditions must be excluded. These include potentially reversible conditions such as depression, adverse drug reactions, metabolic changes, nutritional deficiencies, head injuries and stroke.

Each person with possible Alzheimer's Disease symptoms should have a thorough evaluation. The evaluation should include a complete health history, thorough physical examination, neurological and mental status assessments, and diagnostic tests including blood studies, urinalysis, electrocardiogram and chest x-rays. Other studies often recommended include: computerized tomography (CT Scan), electroencephalography (EEG), removal from medication, format psychiatric assessment, neuropsychological testing, and occasionally, examination of the cerebrospinal fluid by spinal tap. While this evaluation may provide a clinical diagnosis, confirmation of Alzheimer's Disease requires examination of brain tissue, which is usually performed at autopsy.

Treatment:

Although no cure for Alzheimer's Disease is available at present, good planning plus medical and social management can ease the burdens on the patient and family. Appropriate medication can lessen agitation, anxiety and unpredictable behavior, improve sleeping patterns and treat depression. Physical exercise and social activity are important, as are proper nutrition and health maintenance. A calm and well-structured environment may help the afflicted person to maintain as much comfort and dignity as possible.

Next......Stages of Alzheimer's Disease

STAGES OF SYMPTOM PROGRESSION IN ALZHEIMER'S DISEASE

It is difficult to place a patient with Alzheimer's Disease in a specific stage. However, symptoms seem to progress in a recognizable pattern and these stages provide a framework for understanding the disease. It is important to remember they are not uniform in every patient and the stages often overlap.

1. **First Stage - 2 to 4 years leading up to and including diagnosis**

   Symptoms:

   - Recent memory loss begins to affect job performance
   - What was he or she just told to do?
   - Confusion about places--gets lost on way to work
   - Loses spontaneity, the spark or zest for life
   - Mood/personality changes--person becomes anxious about symptoms, avoids people
   - Poor judgement--makes bad decisions
   - Takes longer with routine chores
   - Trouble handling money, paying bills

   Examples:

   - Forgets which bills are paid. Can't remember phone numbers
   - Loses things. Can't remember grocery list
   - Arrives at wrong time or place, or constantly rechecks calendar
   - "Mother's not the same--she's withdrawn, disinterested"
   - She spent all day making dinner and forgot to serve several courses
   - She paid the bills three times over, or didn't pay for three months

2. **Second Stage - 2 - 10 years after diagnosis (longest stage)**

   Symptoms:

   - Increasing memory loss and confusion
   - Shorter attention span
   - Problems recognizing close friends and/or family
   - Repetitive statements and/or movements
   - Restless, especially in late afternoon and at night
   - Occasional muscle twitches or jerking
   - Perceptual motor problems

Continued on Next Page....

Alzheimer's Stages: Continued

- Difficulty organizing thoughts, thinking logically
- Can't find right words--makes up stories to fill in blanks
- Problems with reading, writing and numbers
- May be suspicious, irritable, fidgety, teary or silly
- Loss of impulse control, sloppy, won't bathe or afraid to bathe, trouble dressing
- Gains and then loses weight
- May see or hear things that are not there
- Needs full-time supervision

Examples:

- Can't remember visits immediately after you leave
- Repetitive movements or statements
- Sleeps often; awakens frequently at night and may get up and wander
- Perceptual motor problems, difficulty getting into a chair, setting the table for a meal
- Can't find the right words
- Problems with reading, numbers, can't follow written signs, write name, add or subtract
- Suspicious. May accuse spouse of hiding things, infidelity; may act childish
- Loss of impulse control. Sloppier table manners. May undress at inappropriate times or in the wrong place
- Huge appetite for junk food and other people's food. Forgets when last meal was eaten, then gradually loses interest in food.

3. Terminal Stages - 1 - 3 years

Symptoms:

- Can't recognize family or images of self in mirror
- Loses weight even with good diet
- Little capacity for self care
- Can't communicate with words
- May put everything in mouth or touch everything
- Can't control bowels, bladder
- May have seizures, experiences difficulty with swallowing, skin infections

Examples:

- Looks in mirror and talks to own image
- Needs help with bathing, dressing, eating and toileting
- May groan, scream or make grunting sounds
- May try to suck on everything
- Sleeps more

Alzheimer's: A Summary

WHAT ALZHEIMER'S IS NOT:

- Normal aging

- Hardening of the arteries

- Mental retardation or mental laziness

- A vitamin deficiency

- A direct result of stress, grief, neglect or family conflict

- An emotional illness or a spiritual hex

- Lack of blood or oxygen to the brain

- A result of poisoning, a blow to the head, or chronic alcoholism

- Preventable or curable

- Contagious

WHAT ALZHEIMER'S IS:

- A brain disease causing loss of recent memory, confusion and poor judgement

- A terminal illness that shorten one's expected life span

- A diagnosis of exclusion (after ruling out all other causes of confusion)

- Fourth leading cause of death for American adults

- Costly public health problem

- Confirmed only after death in autopsy

- Tragic for family members and friends

- A drain on family finances, since most long-term care is not covered by private health insurance or Medicare

- Incurable at this time

"The Family Care Roadmap"

- Housing Options
- Home Health Care
- Advanced Planning
- Long Term Care Insurance
- Family Care
- Community Resources
- Extended Care

Thank you.....

For travelling with us on this Family Care journey. We sincerely hope that the information provided through the "Roadmap" is of great benefit both to you and to your older loved ones. (Parents.....Siblings..... Relatives.....)

Please remember, whether you live in Maine, Florida, Washington, California, Texas, etc.....anywhere in this country, it is so important that you:

PLAN....
PREPARE....
ORGANIZE....
COMMUNICATE.....

These are your keys both to Family Care and to Support Networks. It's also "Your Roadmap" to making informed decisions.

End of Tour...
THANKS

NOTES

FOREVER FAMILY
Product Price List

PRODUCT	PRICE Per Unit	QUANTITY	S & H Per Unit	COST
FamilyCare Tool Kit	$89.95		$6.95	
Individual Product Price List				
FamilyCare Organizer (Paperback)	$15.95		$3.95	
FamilyCare Organizer (Hardback/3 ring binder)	$34.95		$4.95	
FamilyCare Roadmap	$17.95		$3.95	
FamilyCare Video Series (Set of 3)	$59.85		$3.95	
FamilyCare Healthbook	$15.95		$3.95	
(Texas Residents Only: Add 8.25% to Product Cost) Sales Tax				
TOTAL COST				

- -

Ordered by _____

Address _____

City _____ State _____ Zip Code _____

Telephone _____

Questions?
Call 1-800-308-8565

Payment:

**Make Checks or
Money Orders payable to:**

**Family Concerns
1340 Main Street Suite #190
Grapevine, Texas   76051**

Credit Card Orders: ❏   Visa   ❏   MasterCard   ❏   American Express

Credit Card #_____ Expiration Date _____

Mail credit card information to above address, or fax credit card information to 817-421-9427

Forever Family

To Order
Call: 1-800-308-8565